Young People's Science Encyclopedia

Ma

Magnifying power
Magnitude
Magnolia
Magpie
Mahogany
Malaria
Malignant
Malleable
Mallow
Malnutrition
Malpighi, Marcello
Mammalia
Mammoth
Mandible
Manganese
Mange
Mango
Mangrove
Man-of-war,
  Portuguese
Manometer
Manure
Manzanita
Maple
Map-making
Marconi, Guglielmo
Marigold
Marijuana
Marine
Marine biology
Marjoram
Marlin
Marmoset
Marmot
Mars
Marsh
Marsupial
Martin
Maser
Mass
Mastodon

Mastoid
Matches
Mathematics
Matter
May fly
Mayer, Maria

Me

Meadowlark
Measles
Measurement
Mechanical
  advantage
Mechanics
Medawar, Peter B.
Median
Medicine
Medulla
Medulla oblongata
Melon
Memory
Mendel, Gregor
  Johann
Mendeleev's
  Periodic Table
Mendelevium
Meninges
Meningitis
Menstruation
Mercury (element)
Mercury (planet)
Meridian
Meristem
Mesa
Meson
Mesozoic Era
Mesquite
Metabolimeter
Metabolism
Metals
Metallurgy
Metamorphosis

Metchnikoff, Elie
Meteor
Methane
Methane series
Metric system

Mi

Mica
Microbe
Microfilm
Microorganism
Microscope
Microscope,
  electron
Microtome
Mid-Atlantic Ridge
Midbrain
Midget
Midnight sun
Migraine
Migration
Migratory cells
Mildew
Milk
Milky Way
Millet
Millibar
Millikan's
  electronic charge
Millipede
Mimicry
Mimosa
Mineral
Mineral water
Mineralogy
Minnow
Mint
Mirage
Mirror
Missile
Mistletoe
Mistral
Mite

Mitosis and meiosis
Mixture

Mo

Mockingbird
Modulus
Moho
Moissan, Henri
Molasses
Mold
Mole
Mole (mammal)
Molecular theory
Molecular weight
Molecule
Mollusca
Molting
Molybdenum
Moment
Momentum
Monel metal
Monera
Mongolism
Mongoose
Monkey
Monocotyledon
Monoecious
Mononucleosis
Monorail
Monotreme
Monsoon
Moon
Moon, phases of
Moor
Moraine
Mordant
Morel
Morning glory
Morphine
Morphology
Morse, Samuel
Moseley, Henry

YOUNG PEOPLE'S
SCIENCE ENCYCLOPEDIA

Edited by the Staff of
NATIONAL COLLEGE OF EDUCATION, Evanston, Illinois

Young People's
SCIENCE
Encyclopedia

Edited by the Staff of
NATIONAL COLLEGE OF EDUCATION
Evanston, Illinois

Volume 11/Ma-Mo

CHILDRENS PRESS ™

CHICAGO

Photographs

Page 2: Skylab space station (NASA)

Page 3: *Top to Bottom:*
Wheatfield (U.S.D.A. Photo)
Technician capping Abbokinase (Abbott Laboratories)
Spider (Macmillan Science Company)
View of Earth (NASA)
Space Shuttle (NASA)
Bahama coral reef (Macmillan Science Company)

Cover: Design by Sandra Gelak
Sumatran Orangutan (San Diego Zoo)
Ocean Experiments (Sea Grant College Program:
University of Delaware)
Halite or Rock Salt (National Teaching Aids, Inc.)

Library of Congress Catalog Card Number: 67-17925

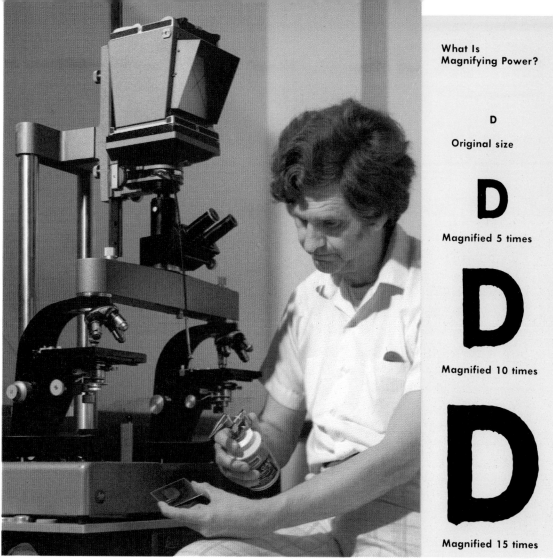

A microscope can magnify objects many times their original size.

What Is Magnifying Power?

D

Original size

D

Magnified 5 times

D

Magnified 10 times

D

Magnified 15 times

Magnifying power A magnifying glass makes objects look larger than they are. The glass is thicker in the middle than it is at its edges. Magnifying power is measured by the number of times larger an object seen through it appears. For example, if an object is 1 inch (2.54 centimeters) tall but through a magnifying glass appears to be 3 inches (7.62 centimeters) tall, the magnifying power is three.

If rays of light reflected from some object are made to pass through a convex lens, an image of that object is formed at a certain distance, or *focal length* from the lens. This depends on the magnifying power of the lens. The shorter the focal length, the greater the magnifying power.

Several convex lenses placed one in front of the other may be used to construct a simple telescope with an even greater magnifying power than that of a single lens. In such an arrangement the front lens, called the *objective lens,* forms an image of the object to be viewed. The second lens, called the *eyepiece,* forms a magnified image of the first image formed by the objective lens. The magnified image formed by the eyepiece is the one seen by the observer. The magnifying power of such combinations of convex lenses is determined by dividing the focal length of the objective lens by the focal length of the eyepiece. Thus, for the greatest magnifying power, the objective lens should have a large focal length and the eyepiece should have a rather short focal length. A. E. L.

SEE ALSO: GLASS; LENS, MAN-MADE; MICROSCOPE

A star of magnitude 1 is 100 times brighter than a star of magnitude 6

Magnitude It is easy to correctly identify a star when both its brightness and its position in the celestial sphere are known. Magnitude is a system of classifying stars according to their brightness as viewed from Earth. This system was first devised by the early Greek astronomers in the second century B.C. At that time only stars that could be seen with the naked eye were classified. The TELESCOPE had not yet been invented.

These astronomers called the brightest stars of the heavens "stars of the first magnitude," and the faintest stars that they could see "stars of the sixth magnitude."

From the early Greek catalogs to modern catalogs and maps of the sky, it has been the custom to express the relative brightness of a star in terms of its magnitude.

With the invention of the telescope, permitting the observation of stars fainter than the sixth magnitude, the number of magnitudes was increased. Greater precision in the measurement of star brightness made it necessary to use decimals to denote the magnitudes. Eventually, a factor slightly greater than 2.5 was adopted as the ratio of brightness corresponding to a difference of 1 magnitude. Therefore, a star of magnitude 3.0 is about 2½ times as bright as a star of magnitude 4.0. The lower the magnitude number, the brighter the star. Negative numbers are also used in the modern system of classification. A star with magnitude of -1 is brighter than a star of magnitude $+1$.

The brightness of a star as seen from earth depends on its *luminosity* and its distance from earth. *Absolute magnitude* is the actual brightness at a distance of 10 *parsecs* (a parsec is 3.26 light-years).   H. S. G.

SEE ALSO: CONSTELLATIONS

Magnolia in bloom

Magnolia (magg-NOHL-yuh) LEAVES of the magnolia tree are large, simple, dark-green, and leathery. Some are evergreen. Magnolia range in size from 4 inches (10.16 centimeters) to 3 feet (0.91 meters). The FLOWERS are white, pink, or red.

The Magnoliaceae family was named after Pierre Magnol, the first taxonomist to group plants into families. It contains about 100 species. The cucumber tree is an evergreen with green, bell-shaped flowers. It produces three-inch (7.62 centimeters), cucumber-shaped, green fruit covered with red seeds. The umbrella tree is non-evergreen or *deciduous*. White cup-shaped flowers mature into a two- to four-inch (5.08 to 10.16 centimeters) rosy fruit. Mountain magnolia has yellow blossoms and a red, cone-shaped fruit. Bigleaf, sweet-bay, and earleaf are other species.

Flowers are bisexual, large, and solitary; they have numerous petals and sepals which are often similar in size and color. Stamens and pistils are numerous. The flower cluster matures into a compound FRUIT classified as aggregates of follicles or samaras.   H.J.C.

Magpie The American magpie is the only large black and white bird with a very long tail. It lives in western North America. Its head and back are black. The tail is metallic green. The bill is black and wing patches and belly are white. A California species is similar except for a yellow bill and a bare yellow spot behind the eye.

Magpie

Magpies are intelligent birds, capable of learning to talk. They are also pests because they destroy the young and eggs of other birds, eat chickens, and attack weak or injured stock. Since they feed in flocks, they can do considerable damage to an area.

These birds use the same nest every year and mate for life. They nest in brush, building a covered nest with two entrances. The twig roof protects them from hawks. Six to nine grayish-green eggs smudged with brown are laid and incubated by the female.   J. C. K.

Mahogany tree, flower and wood

Mahogany It is a hardwood tree which grows 40 to 50 feet (12.19 to 15.24 meters) high. Many leaflets make up a single evergreen leaf. FLOWERS are single and white. FRUIT develops from a fleshy stalk and from the flower ovary. It is an accessory fruit.

Mahogany trees grow in tropical America. There are three kinds—African, West Indian, and Honduras mahogany. They are members of the family Meliaceae.

The heavy, reddish-brown wood is strong and durable. The crooked grain takes a high polish. Lumber is expensive, for many stands of trees are deep in jungles and difficult to harvest. Furniture is often made of a cheaper base with a veneer of mahogany.   H. J. C.

Maidenhair tree see Ginkgo

Maize see Corn

Malachite see Copper

Malaria (muh-LAIR-ee-uh) Malaria is a sickness caused by an animal PARASITE which is visible only under a microscope. This animal parasite has the generic name *Plasmodium.* It is transferred to people by the bite of an infected MOSQUITO.

Anopheles mosquito, a carrier of malaria

Malaria shows itself by an attack of chills, followed by a fever and then a sweat. The attacks may occur daily, every other day, or with three days in between. Each type of the disease is caused by a *Plasmodium* with an additional species name, but all are members of the same genus and all need to reside for a time in the mosquito to complete a phase of their development.

Because of this relationship with the mosquito, the disease is more prevalent in swampy places. Malaria was well-known in Rome because the marshes around the city provided excellent breeding grounds. The Italians named the disease malaria because of their mistaken notion that bad air was the only cause. Their word "mal", meaning bad, and "aria", meaning air, shows that they lacked knowledge of the disease.

It was not until the nineteenth century that more accurate knowledge of the disease finally was gained. The work of PASTEUR and KOCH did away almost completely with the "bad air" theory and tended to fortify the belief that small animals got into man's blood stream and were carried from one person to another by means of bites from the mosquitos of swamps and marshes.

The use of Peruvian bark or cinchona proved a treatment for the disease. Refinement of the drug into the present-day QUININE has been of great value to man. Today quinine and, more especially, its synthetic substitutes such as *atabrine* are used as preventive measures.   H. K. S.

Male see Heredity; Reproduction, sexual

Malignant Malignant is a term describing either a deadly disease or a TUMOR or growth. A malignant growth usually spreads rapidly, and, unless removed by surgery, by radioactive treatment, or by drugs (CHEMOTHERAPY), it may cause death.

SEE ALSO: CANCER (DISEASE)

Mallard see Ducks

Malleable (MAHL-ee-uh-buhl) Malleable refers to metal and means the METAL is able to be hammered, pressed or rolled out into a thin sheet or other shape without being broken. GOLD is by far the most malleable metal.

Malleus see Ear

Mallow Mallow is the name of a garden flower, a genus of plants and a plant family. Leaves are usually lobed and alternate. Flower parts are in fives. They are white or pink to red. The fruit is often a capsule. Roots contain much mucilage. There are annuals, biennials and perennials. Some species bearing the name are *musk mallow, rose mallow* and the *common mallow,* which is a weed. COTTON is a mallow.

Purple althea, a shrub mallow

Malnutrition Malnutrition results when the body does not receive the correct amounts or the right kinds of food. Malnutrition may occur in animals (including man) as well as plants. When the body is in a state of malnutrition, it becomes susceptible to disease and infection.

Malnutrition may be caused by failure of the body to absorb the nutrients in proper food. A common example of this is the loss of food by chronic or recurring DIARRHEA.

Malnutrition occurs in individuals or in groups of people because of poverty, famine, wars, disease, or ignorance.

The body must obtain a mixture of fats, carbohydrates, proteins, water, vitamins, and minerals to remain healthy. Plentiful food supplies lacking one or more of these necessary ingredients may cause a form of malnutrition known as *hidden hunger.*

Widespread food shortages resulting in malnutrition and starvation in large groups of people are called *famines.* War caused a famine in Kampuchea (Cambodia) in the late 1970s. In the 1980s and 1990s, war and droughts have caused a number of famines in Africa. In 1992 and 1993, many nations worked to bring relief to famine victims in the African nation of Somalia.   J.K.K./J.H.

SEE ALSO: ANOREXIA, CARBOHYDRATES, FAT, MINERALS, NUTRITION, PROTEIN, VITAMIN

Malpighi, Marcello (mal-PEEG-he) (1628-1694) Malpighi was an Italian physiologist who founded *microscopic* ANATOMY. By using his microscope, he was the first medical researcher to trace the complete circuit of BLOOD in the human body. Vitally interested in the study of insects, Malpighi made, at the request of The Royal Society of London, a superb special study of the anatomy of the silkworm. While he was studying insects microscopically, he discovered in insects and other animals what is now known as the *Malpighian tube* which removes wastes from the body cavity and passes them into the alimentary canal.

Born near Bologna, Italy, Malpighi studied medicine at the University of Bologna. Three years after he graduated, he became a lecturer and several months later was appointed professor of theoretical medicine at the University of Pisa. He remained there four years before returning to the University of Bologna. Then he accepted a post at Messina for four years, after which he returned once again to Bologna. This time he remained for twenty-five years. When he was sixty-three, Malpighi moved to Rome to become the personal physician to Pope Innocent XII. He died at the Vatican on November 30, 1694.   D. H. J.

SEE ALSO: MEDICINE

Mammalia (mam-MAY-lyuh) All people have seen mother cats feed their kittens. These tiny animals drink milk from a small nipple or swelling on the mother's body. The word *mamma* means "mother." Like the mother cats, all female mammals feed their young with their own milk.

People are mammals. In fact, most of the largest and best-known animals in the world are mammals. Most of them live on land. However, a few, like the sea cow and the WALRUS, live in the ocean. The smallest mammal is the tiny SHREW, which weighs less than an ounce (28.35 grams). The largest is the blue WHALE, which weighs 120 tons (108.84 metric tons). Although most land mammals move by jumping, running, or walking on land, the bat is able to fly. Some, like the DUCKBILL, even lay eggs.

Like people, all mammals breathe with LUNGS. Even the whale must come to the surface of the ocean to take in air. Also, mammals have skin covered with hair. The ELEPHANT has only a few hairs, while the bear has a heavy fur coat. Others have unusual hair. The quills of a PORCUPINE are really very large hairs. The horns of a RHINOCEROS are made of thousands of tiny hairs packed together.

Mammals have been divided into three main groups, according to the way the young mammals are born and nursed. *Monotremes,* or egg-laying mammals, are the most unusual. The duckbills and SPINY ANTEATERS are the only types belonging to this group. The eggs are laid and incubated outside the mother's body.

The *marsupials,* or pouched mammals, are one of the most interesting. Included in this group are the KOALA bear, WOMBAT, KANGAROO—all found chiefly in Australia—and the OPOSSUM of North America. The young are born in a partly-developed state

Macmillan Science Company
Mammals produce milk to feed their young.

and they find their way into a large pouch on the belly of the female. They attach themselves to nipples inside the pouch and remain until they are more mature.

The *placental mammals* form the largest group, since they include 95% of all living mammals. During PREGNANCY the females develop a special organ, called the *placenta.* Part of the placenta is formed from the outer membranous sac around the embryo and part of it comes from the mucosa of the uterus. This organ passes nourishment from the mother's body to the fetus, or embryo, which is attached to the placenta by an umbilical cord. Thus, the young develop inside the body of the mother.

The placental mammals are divided into a number of orders. The major ones are described below.

The order Insectivora includes the shrew, mole, and hedgehog. They are small primitive mammals with a long, tapered snout. Their diet consists mainly of insects, and they are nocturnal.

The order Edentata includes the armadillo, anteater, and sloth. They have large front claws and most of them lack teeth. The few that have teeth are missing the enamel and roots.

The order Rodentia includes the rat, squirrel, porcupine, guinea pig, hamster, chipmunk, beaver, chinchilla, and woodchuck. They are chiefly herbivores. They have one pair of large incisors in each jaw. These teeth keep growing as they are worn down from gnawing.

The order Lagomorpha includes the hare, rabbit, and pika. These animals were once classified as rodents because they are herbivores and their incisors grow continually. Since they have two pair of upper incisors, they were placed in a separate order.

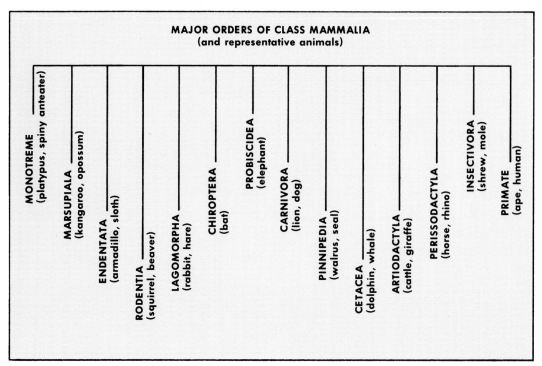

MAJOR ORDERS OF CLASS MAMMALIA
(and representative animals)

MONOTREME (platypus, spiny anteater)

MARSUPIALA (kangaroo, opossum)

ENDENTATA (armadillo, sloth)

RODENTIA (squirrel, beaver)

LAGOMORPHA (rabbit, hare)

CHIROPTERA (bat)

PROBISCIDEA (elephant)

CARNIVORA (lion, dog)

PINNIPEDIA (walrus, seal)

CETACEA (dolphin, whale)

ARTIODACTYLA (cattle, giraffe)

PERISSODACTYLA (horse, rhino)

INSECTIVORA (shrew, mole)

PRIMATE (ape, human)

Only the flying mammals are classified in the order of Chiroptera. These are all the bat families. They are nocturnal and possess very sharp teeth. Their wings are formed from webbed forelimbs.

The dolphin, porpoise, and whale are in the order Cetacea. These aquatic mammals have front legs that are paddle-like and are called flippers. They have hair only around the muzzle, a thick layer of blubber under the skin, and one or two nostrils on top of the head, referred to as a blowhole.

The Carnivora order includes the dog, cat, bear, fox, racoon, wolf, hyena, lion, tiger, mink, skunk, weasel, and otter. They have well-developed canines, which are large pointed teeth to tear their prey. They usually have five claws on each foot.

The members in the order Pinnipedia were once classified with the carnivores. These mammals are the walrus, seal, and sea lion. They are aquatic animals with flippers, large eyes, and greatly reduced ears.

The only animal today in the order Proboscidea is the elephant. The mammoth and the mastodon are extinct. Elephants have a trunk formed from an elongated upper lip and nose. They have a thin coat of hair, tough and loose skin, large ears, and tusks formed from two upper incisors.

The even-toed hoofed mammals are classified in the order Artiodactyla. These include cattle, swine, sheep, camel, hippopotamus, deer, goat, giraffe, and bison. Many of them are *ruminants,* having several stomachs. They usually have two toes on each foot and horns or antlers.

The odd-toed hoofed mammals are in the order Perissodactyla. They include the horse, donkey, rhinoceros, tapir, mule, ass, and zebra. They all possess a simple stomach and were once classified with the other hoofed mammals as Ungulates. Many animals in this group are extinct today.

Finally, the most advanced order is the Primate. Included in this group are the monkey, lemur, marmoset, gorilla, chimpanzee, gibbon, orangutan, and humans. They have an opposable thumb which is adapted for grasping. They have a large cerebrum, and many species stand erect.

All mammals are warm-blooded; that is, the temperature of the body remains the same, regardless of external temperature.

All mammals have a DIAPHRAGM, which aids in breathing. This large muscular sheet divides the chest cavity from the abdominal cavity. As the diaphragm contracts and relaxes, it enlarges and decreases the size of the chest cavity.

Since they have a well-developed internal SKELETON, with the spinal cord surrounded by vertebrae, all mammals are vertebrates. Because many bones have fused together, the skeleton is simpler than that of lower chordates. For example, the skull of the bony fish may contain over 170 bones, whereas the skull of man has only 8.

An outstanding feature of mammals, particularly of man, is the large size of the BRAIN. Also, the surface of the mammal brain is covered with many folds. E.P.L./H.J.C.

SEE ALSO: ANIMALS, CLASSIFICATION OF; MARSUPIAL; REPRODUCTION, SEXUAL.

Chicago Natural History Museum
Mammoths are the ancestors of the Indian elephant.

Mammoth The mammoth was a relative of the ELEPHANT. It is now extinct and is found only as a fossil. It lived many thousands of years ago when the saber-toothed tiger also lived.

Most of the characteristics of the mammoth were identical to the Indian elephant. One difference was its thick, dark brown hair, sometimes 2 feet (.61 meters) long. The elephant has just a little short hair spread over its body. The long hair made the mammoth look larger than it was. It also had short, furry ears and a special spiral tusk that elephants do not have.

The scientific name of the mammoth is *Elephas primigenius,* which means "first-born elephant." The species lived all over the Northern Hemisphere. Cave drawings by the Cro-Magnon men 10,000 years ago show that the mammoth was hunted for its meat. The word "Behemoth" in the Bible refers to the mammoth.

The great mystery about the mammoth is how it became extinct. Masses of bones, complete skeletons, and whole quick-frozen animals have been found, especially in the TUNDRA of northern Siberia. One specimen, known as the *Beresovka mammoth,* had buttercups in its mouth indicating that it had died and been frozen instantly without warning. Although it had been hidden under snow and ice for 10,000 years, its meat, when thawed, was still tasty. One of the great problems of the paleontologists has been to discover how such perfect preservation could occur.   J. F. B.

SEE ALSO: FOSSILS, PALEONTOLOGY

Man see Anthropology, Evolution, Evolution of man, Human being, Mammalia, Primates

Mandible A mandible is an organ associated with the mouth and usually used for biting. The upper and lower beaks of birds, the lower jawbone of mammals and the jawlike seizing and biting organs of many insects are all mandibles.

SEE: INSECTA, SKELETON

Mandibles of birds, insects and mammals appear very different even though they have a similar function

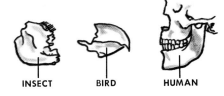

INSECT   BIRD   HUMAN

Manganese (MANG-guh-nees) Manganese is a useful hard gray metal. Not a very common element, manganese makes up less than 0.1% of the earth's crust. When it is added to STEEL, it increases the hardness and strength of the steel.

Black powdered manganese dioxide has wide use as a CATALYST and absorbing chemical. It is used in dry cells.

Manganese is included in a group of elements called *transition* elements. They are classified together because in chemical changes electrons are added to inner rather than outer shells of their atoms.

Manganese (symbol Mn) is element number 25. Its atomic weight is 54.938.

J. R. S.

SEE ALSO: ATOM, ELEMENTS

Mange (MAYNJ) Mange is a skin disease which affects certain domestic animals such as dogs, cats, horses, and pigs. It is caused by tiny MITES which burrow into the skin, hair follicles, or sweat glands. Itching and scratching often followed by INFECTION results.

Mango

Mango

Mango The mango is one of the oldest trees grown by man, perhaps for 6000 years. It is a sacred tree and a basic fruit in India. One must build up a liking for it. One variety is reported to have the flavor of turpentine.

Mango trees need alternate dry and wet periods for growth. The leaves are dark and shiny and the flowers are light orange-red. The fruit, classed as a drupe, has a juicy, fibrous pulp around a large, oval seed. The fruit turns greenish yellow or orange when ripe and may weigh as much as 5 pounds (2.27 kilograms).

The mango tree attracts a species of fruit fly which harms crops in the United States, so importing and growing is limited. **H. J. C.**

Mangrove (MANG-grohv) Mangrove is a tropical evergreen tree that grows in calm salt waters of bays and river mouths. Roots grow from the trunk-like *stilts* forming a tangled network which collects mud and forms land.

Dredging of some southern U.S. coastal waters has upset the balance of mildly salty waters mangrove trees require, starting heated debate in the 1990s. Thousands of acres of mangrove swamps have been filled in for urban development. **J.H.**

SEE: PLANTS, TROPICAL

Manila hemp see Hemp

Mangrove

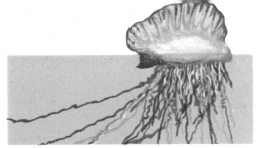

Portuguese man-of-war

Man-of-war, Portuguese Portuguese man-of-war, or *Physalia,* is a colony of animals found on the surface of warm seas. Instead of being attached, the colony develops a large, crested gas bag, or *float*. The crest on the float acts as a sail. The colony is moved by wind or water currents.

Hanging from the float is a colony made of several kinds of *polyps,* or individuals. They are long, tentacled individuals that protect the colony and capture food. Some of these tentacles may be over 60 feet (18.29 meters) long. They bear stinging cells called *nematocysts* which paralyze prey. After the prey is paralyzed, the tentacles contract and draw the animal up toward the float where feeding polyps digest it.

There are also bell-shaped, medusa-like individuals. They are reproductive polyps, producing eggs and sperm. **J. C. K.**
SEE ALSO: COELENTERATA

Manometer (muh-NAHM-uh-tuhr) A manometer is an instrument for measuring pressure of gases. It usually consists of a U-shaped tube with both arms open. Mercury is at the bottom of the U and slightly up in the arms. When a gas with a pressure higher than the pressure of the atmosphere enters one arm, the mercury moves up the other arm, indicating the pressure of the gas by the amount it moves.

Manta ray see Ray

Manure There are two types of manure—animal and green. Digestive wastes (excretions) from poultry and mammals are called animal manure. Green manure is when crops are plowed under instead of being harvested.

Manure is used as a natural fertilizer. It increases the population of bacteria and fungi vital for decomposition. Manure promotes water retention and aeration. It returns nitrogen, phosphoric acid, and potash to the soil.

Tons of manure from feedlots in cattle country go to waste, with much of it washing into waterways. Researchers are currently working on the idea of using manure as a future source of energy.   H.J.C.

Manzanita (mann-zuh-NEE-tuh) About 50 kinds of evergreen trees and shrubs are in the manzanita group. The *bear-berry* is a trailing shrub of the northern U.S. with light-pink flowers in clusters. The fruit is a red drupe with several nutlets.

Maple The maple tree provides shade, valuable wood, maple sugar, and beautiful colors in autumn. Maple leaves are shaped like the palm of a hand (palmate) with sharp-toothed edges. They grow opposite each other in pairs. The maple tree bears fruit with little wings so the wind can scatter the seeds.

In America, the best-known maple is the *rock* or *sugar maple*. It is a stately, round-headed, gray-barked tree which may grow 120 feet (36.58 meters) high. Noted for its rich red colors in fall, the sugar maple is prized by cabinet makers for its wavy-grained wood. It is also the most important maple for its maple sugar yield.   J.K.K.

SEE ALSO: LEAVES, LUMBER, SUGARS

Sugar maple (left) and silver maple (right)

Map-making The making of maps is a part of the science of geography. This division of geography is called *cartography*. Thousands of years ago, the people of the Mediterranean area began to devise maps of the parts of the earth with which they were familiar.

The truest map of the earth is the globe because it is spherical and nearly the shape of the earth. The first globe of the earth was made about the time Columbus discovered America. Long before this, maps were made on flat paper, but usually these maps were of only a small part of the earth's surface.

The most difficult problem faced by a cartographer is trying to show a spherical earth on a flat surface. There have been many different types of *projections* developed. A map projection is an orderly system of parallels and meridians drawn upon a flat surface. These parallels and meridians represent the earth's geographic grid. No single map projection of any type can present a true picture of the earth's surface, though some come closer than others.

A list of all the kinds of map projections is quite large, but three general types may be identified. These types are *geometric, perspective,* and *globe-skin*. Each type has certain advantages, but all introduce some kind of distortion, especially when large areas of the earth's surface are covered. The errors found on flat maps are errors in direction, shape, and area. One or more of these distortions occur on all map projections.

Geometric projections include *cylindrical* projections of which the *Mercator* map is the best known. This map is a modified cylindrical projection. The map is made by wrapping a cylinder of paper around the globe, transferring the earth's features onto a cylinder, and unrolling the cylinder to show the earth on a rectangular sheet. The meridians and lines of parallel are shown as straight lines. This map is good for *navigation* because it shows true direction, but it becomes badly distorted near the poles. For example, Greenland looks much

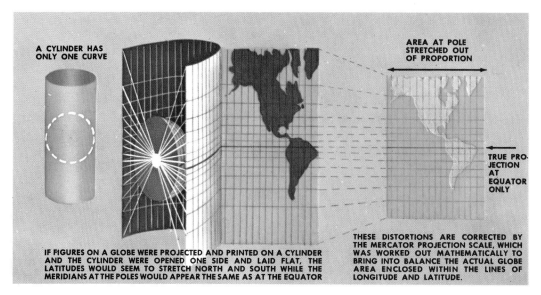

A CYLINDER HAS ONLY ONE CURVE

AREA AT POLE STRETCHED OUT OF PROPORTION

TRUE PROJECTION AT EQUATOR ONLY

IF FIGURES ON A GLOBE WERE PROJECTED AND PRINTED ON A CYLINDER AND THE CYLINDER WERE OPENED ONE SIDE AND LAID FLAT, THE LATITUDES WOULD SEEM TO STRETCH NORTH AND SOUTH WHILE THE MERIDIANS AT THE POLES WOULD APPEAR THE SAME AS AT THE EQUATOR

THESE DISTORTIONS ARE CORRECTED BY THE MERCATOR PROJECTION SCALE, WHICH WAS WORKED OUT MATHEMATICALLY TO BRING INTO BALANCE THE ACTUAL GLOBE AREA ENCLOSED WITHIN THE LINES OF LONGITUDE AND LATITUDE.

larger than the continent of Australia.

Another geometric projection is the *conic,* made by placing a cone over the globe and transferring those parts of the earth onto the paper cone. When the cone is cut and flattened out, the map is a flat hemisphere in shape. Some maps of Europe are made this way. The scale is true along the line of contact of the cone with the globe. Conic projections show only a small distortion of shape and area. *Lambert's conformal* projection cuts off the apex of the cone and part of the bottom. The remaining parts of the cone show very little distortion when unrolled.

Perspective projections are somewhat like the eye perspective in drawing. If a drawing is made of the earth when the globe is viewed from a distance, the result would be a perspective map. Of course, such a map shows only half the earth. Measurement on these maps is rather difficult because the three-dimensional half-globe becomes a two-dimensional flat map. The point of view controls the appearance of the earth. For example, if the point of view were from the center of the earth to the outer surface, the projection would be badly distorted in area and shape. This is called a *Gnomonic* projection. It may be called a geometric type because it is projected onto a plane held in contact with the globe at the equator.

The third type of projection may be called *globe-skin,* although specific types are called by a variety of names. Globe-skin maps are made by taking a replica of half of the earth and flattening it, like the example of half an orange. The splits which occur are called *gores.* Some of these are squeezed together. A variation of this method is the *Interrupted Homolosine* projection where the splits which are left are generally placed over the water areas of the oceans.

Today, *polar* projections are becoming increasingly important. They are useful in air navigation because *great circle* routes over the north pole are the shortest routes connecting the great land masses of the Northern Hemisphere. This projection is made by centering a plane surface over the pole and transferring the earth's features onto the flat surface. Distortions become great at distances away from the polar zone.

Accurate map reading requires care. The grid lines, parallels and meridians are necessary to read longitude and latitude. Only by reading these can the true direction from one place to another be determined. For example, on some projections the lines of parallel may be curved instead of straight, and a location which appears to be northwest of another may be actually due west when the line of parallel is followed. Often the scales of distance are correct only along a certain line of parallel. Latitude (in degrees) is measured north and south of the equator along meridian lines. Longitude is measured east and west from the prime meridian along lines of parallel. C. L. K.

SEE ALSO: EARTH, GEOGRAPHY

Marble see Rocks

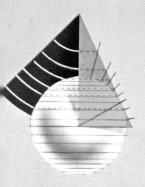

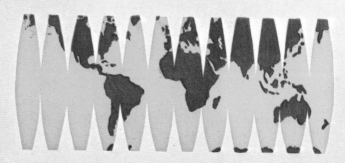

TERRESTRIAL GLOBES ARE MADE FROM A FLAT PATTERN. TWELVE GORES AND TWO POLAR CAPS ARE OUTLINED, THE MAP IS PRINTED ON A FLAT SURFACE, THEN CUT AND CAREFULLY MOLDED TO A SPHERE.

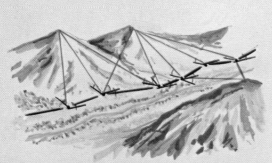

GROUND MAPS START WITH STATE SURVEYS TO MEAS-URE THE PEAKS AND VALLEYS. THE UNITS OF ELEVA-TION ARE CALLED "BENCHES"

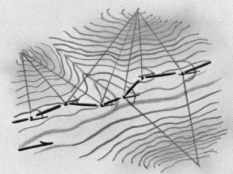

BENCHES ARE SHOWN ON THE FINISHED MAP AS LINES FOLLOWING THE CONTOUR OF THE LAND. A STEEP SLOPE WOULD BE SHOWN AS HAVING THE LINES CLOSE TOGETHER

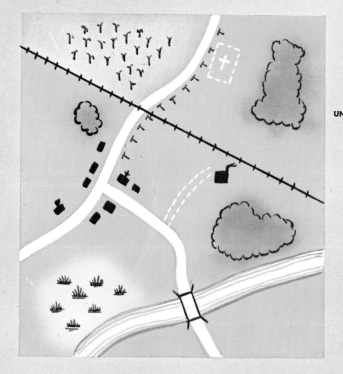

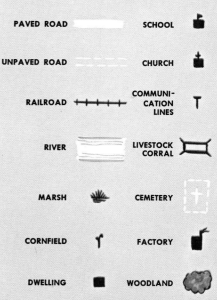

AERIAL MAP AND LEGEND GIVING SYMBOLS

PAVED ROAD		SCHOOL
UNPAVED ROAD		CHURCH
RAILROAD		COMMUNI-CATION LINES
RIVER		LIVESTOCK CORRAL
MARSH		CEMETERY
CORNFIELD		FACTORY
DWELLING		WOODLAND

Guglielmo Marconi

Marconi, Guglielmo (mahr-KOH-nee, gool-YEL-moh) (1874-1937) Marconi was the inventor of wireless telegraphy; that is, radio broadcasting by means of a dot-and-dash code, which is still used for certain purposes. It was the forerunner of broadcasting by voice, as is now used in commercial radio.

Born in Bologna, Italy, of an Italian father and an Irish mother, Marconi and his brother were educated by tutors at home. Later, Marconi attended the University of Bologna. He was only twenty when he had his great idea for sending signals with electrical waves.

When Marconi was sixteen, he successfully proved his theory that an electric current can pass through most substances without difficulty. He also demonstrated that an electric current will travel in a direct course without a conductor if it is started in a particular direction.

When he was twenty-two, Marconi obtained a British patent on his first sending and receiving system. To make it, he had built

on the work of many scientists, including Hertz, whose theory of electrical waves had set him thinking about the possibility of transmitting them. Marconi was the first to see how all these ideas could be put together to make a workable wireless set, although many others had tried.

The Italian government was not interested in his work, and in 1895 he went to England and founded the Marconi Company, employing some top experts to help him. He soon invented *tuning,* which made it possible to have many different stations without their interfering with each other. The famous British Patent No. 7777 was granted for this tuning system.

The following year, wireless began to be installed in the lighthouses along the English coast. The *Goodwin Sands* lightship, struck by a storm in 1899, used wireless to obtain help. The *Titanic* disaster in 1912 gave the wireless even more fame. Those who survived were rescued by ships that had received the wireless call of the sinking ship.

In 1901, Marconi tried sending a message across the Atlantic Ocean. Mathematicians did not believe that radio waves could go so far because of the curvature of the earth, but Marconi proved them wrong. From a sending station built in Cornwall, England, he transmitted a letter *S* to a receiving station near St. John's, Newfoundland. The antenna on his receiving station was held up by a kite, for he had proved early in his career that the higher the aerial, the farther the waves will travel.

As early as 1922, Marconi saw the importance of short waves, and anticipated the development of RADAR. He found that radio waves were reflected from metal objects, and suggested that they could be used to detect the presence of ships in fog even if those ships did not have RADIO.

Marconi, who spoke English as well as he spoke Italian, made several visits to the United States. He won the Nobel Prize and many other honors.   M. R. B.
SEE ALSO: SOUND, SHORT-WAVE RADIO

Mare see Baby animals, Horse

Marigold (MAIR-ih-gold) Marigolds are yellow or orange flowers, called *marigold* because of their golden color. They are annual plants grown each year from seed.

French monarch marigold

Courtesy Society For
Visual Education, Inc.

Mart Toggweiler

A garibaldi peering out of a rock crevice guarded by a starfish

African varieties are from 2½ to 4 feet (0.76 to 1.22 meters) tall. The French marigolds are from 9 inches to 2½ feet (22.86 centimeters to .76 meters) tall. The dwarf marigolds, grown in pots or used for garden borders, are from 9 to 12 inches (22.86 to 30.48 centimeters) tall. Shakespeare called the pot marigolds "winking Mary-buds." The flower heads close at night and open in the sunlight.

The *bur marigold* is a wild flower, 5 feet (1.52 meters) high with small orange flowers. The burs irritate the skin of sheep and other animals.   P.G.B.

Marijuana (mah-ruh-HWAHN-uh) Marijuana is a drug that stimulates people. It is presently against the law to use it. The drug is obtained from the leaves and flowers of the hemp plant. This plant is usually raised to obtain fibers for rope and other products. Indian hemp and plants similar to it have been known and used since ancient times.

The leaves of the hemp plant are dried and shredded to make marijuana. It is smoked as cigarettes. The sale of marijuana is often associated with organized crime. A person under the influence of marijuana may have a variety of reactions, ranging from over-gaiety and talkativeness to extreme silence and pensiveness.

Studies are being conducted to determine exactly what the long-term physical effects of marijuana might be. Some people who smoke marijuana eventually go on to become addicted to stronger drugs.

The raising of the hemp plant is strictly regulated in the United States. In many states the use of marijuana is illegal.

Marine Marine is a word which originated with the Latin word *mare,* meaning "sea." It is used as an adjective to show that certain terms have to do with the sea or ocean.

Marine biology The study of living ocean creatures is called *marine biology*. Along the ocean shore, there are many delightful plants and animals. SNAILS creep slowly along the sand, leaving tiny tracks. CRAYFISH hide themselves under rocks. Tiny sandworms pop their heads out of holes. The gardens of SEAWEED disappear as the waves roll over them. The ocean is a home for many kinds of plants and animals. Those on the dark ocean bottom are just as interesting as those on the shore.

The study of life in the deep ocean has been difficult. However, with new instruments for drilling and dredging the ocean floor, many new discoveries have been made. Scientists used to think that plants and animals could not live below a certain depth. But wherever they have explored, they have found living creatures. While a great deal is known about life in the ocean, much still remains a mystery.

ENVIRONMENTS OF THE OCEAN

The ocean basin is shaped like a hat, turned upside down. The *continental shelf* forms the brim of the hat. From the coastline, it slopes gently downward for a distance of 100 miles (161 kilometers) and ends at the continen-

The plants and animals of the benthic zone are adapted to hold on to rocks against tidal action; for example, organisms in a tide pool (left), fanworms (center), and shoreline snails (right)

tal slope. The slope, like the side of the hat, drops off sharply for many thousand feet (meters) and ends at the *abyssal plain* or ocean bed. The abyssal plain, which forms the top of the hat, is a long horizontal area covered, like land, with high mountains and deep trenches.

In this ocean basin, there are two main types of environment. The ocean floor, from the shoreline to the bottom of the trenches, is called the *benthic zone. Benthos* is Greek for "depth of the sea." Plants and animals living in this area are called *benthic organisms*. Benthic animals are chiefly invertebrates, which creep or crawl or attach themselves to the bottom. Benthic plants are mainly the ALGAE, found along the shoreline, which cling to rocks and firm ground.

The water itself, which fills the ocean basin forms the *pelagic zone*. This term is taken from the Greek word meaning "sea." The organisms in this area are, of course, free to move through the water, either by drifting or swimming.

In the pelagic zone, the sun's rays penetrate the water to a depth ranging from 250 to 600 feet (76.2 to 182.88 meters). Organisms which live in this sunlit area are called PLANKTON, which means "wandering." Since most of them are microscopic in size, they drift helplessly with the waves and currents.

Below the lighted surface, there is eternal night. Animals in this part of the pelagic zone are called *nekton,* which means "swimming." Most of them are strong swimmers, able to make their way against the currents. Actually, these animals are found in nearly every area of the ocean, from the deepest waters to the surface.

While ocean plants and animals are classified according to the environment in which they live, they are also classified according to evolutionary origin. Members of almost every phylum of animals are found in the ocean. Some phyla, such as the sponges, coelenterates, mollusks, and echinoderms, are almost completely marine. The plant phyla are poorly represented, since the majority of ocean plants belong to the algae.

LIFE ON THE OCEAN FLOOR
(BENTHIC ZONE)

The heaviest populations of organisms are found close to the shore. Since air, land and water meet with great force, the shoreline has the most violent climate on the earth. As the tide rises and falls, organisms are exposed to drying, flooding, baking, and freezing. Most animals are streamlined or flattened, so that water rolls easily over them. Many, like the BARNACLE and snail, withdraw into a shell. The WORMS and CRABS burrow under the sand. SEA URCHINS and sponges find shelter in rock hollows. Seaweeds anchor themselves to rocks by means of a root-like process, called a *holdfast.*

Below the tide level, there are dense communities of plants and animals. The continental shelf is a desirable area, since plants are able to attach themselves to the ocean bottom as well as remain within the range of sunlight. Plants, in turn, attract many animals. However, along the continental slope, where there is little sunlight, the organisms decrease in number and size. Even in the thick mud and sand of the abyssal plain, entire communities of living creatures have recently been discovered.

LIFE IN THE SURFACE WATERS
(UPPER PELAGIC ZONE)

Since green plants need sunlight in order

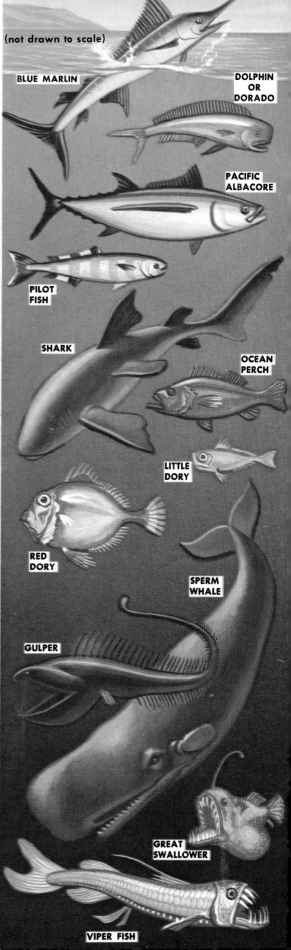

(not drawn to scale)

BLUE MARLIN

DOLPHIN OR DORADO

PACIFIC ALBACORE

PILOT FISH

SHARK

OCEAN PERCH

LITTLE DORY

RED DORY

SPERM WHALE

GULPER

GREAT SWALLOWER

VIPER FISH

to manufacture food, they are confined to the upper surface of the pelagic zone. The plants, which are called *phytoplankton,* consist mainly of algae, many of which give a particular color to the ocean surface. The animals, which are called *zooplankton,* contain members of nearly every phylum. There are many PROTOZOA and crustaceans, in addition to the larva and eggs of larger animals. Phytoplankton is an important food in the ocean. It is eaten by the zooplankton as well as by larger animals.

LIFE IN THE DEEP WATERS
(LOWER PELAGIC ZONE)

While there may be drastic changes, such as volcanic eruptions and current shifts, weather and seasonal changes are almost absent there. The deep waters are very cold. Water pressure increases steadily with depth.

The deep ocean is one of the most competitive environments in the world. Many animals come to the surface at night to feed on plankton. However, others feed upon smaller animals or dead organisms, which drift down from the upper waters. Food is scarce and meals come at irregular intervals.

Apart from the mollusks, like the OCTOPUS and SQUID, the invertebrates are poorly represented in this area. However, there are many large vertebrates. Bony fish, like the TUNA, cartilaginous fish like the skates and sharks, air-breathing mammals like the WHALE and SEAL, reptiles like the sea serpent and TURTLE, travel these waters. Most of them are dark in color so that they merge with their surroundings.

In the pitch-black world of the abyssal plain, the animals are weird in appearance. Most of them are small, scaleless, and flabby. Many have developed enormous teeth and mouths. Others are without eyes, while some have eyes which bulge like golf balls. Some have luminescent spots or filaments, which glow in the dark. Since the problem of finding a mate in the black waters is difficult, one species of fish has solved the problem. The male lives permanently attached to the female. Scientists believe that bacteria provide an important food source for deep water animals. E. P. L.

SEE ALSO: COELENTERATA, CRUSTACEA, ECHINODERMATA, FISH, MOLLUSCA, OCEAN, OCEANOGRAPHY, PORIFERA, REPTILIA

Mariposa see Lily

Marmoset

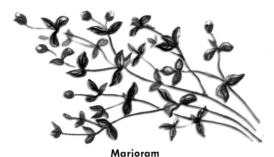

Marjoram

Marjoram (MAHR-johr-um) Marjoram is an herb with tender leaves, stem and flowers. As with many other mint plants, the dried plant parts are used for flavoring. Oil is removed from the plant and used in perfumes and soaps.

Sweet marjoram is an annual, native to the Mediterranean region. The stem reaches a height of 2 feet (.61 meters). The leaves are small and opposite. The white or purple flower appears in later summer.

The *pot marjoram* is an erect perennial. The oval opposite leaves are 1 inch (2.54 centimeters) long. Flowers are pink.

Wild marjoram, a perennial originally from Europe, is sometimes called *oregano,* but botanically OREGANO is classified as a separate species.   H.J.C.

Marlin The largest of the three species of marlin in North America is the blue marlin. It can weigh 1,000 pounds (453 kilograms). Marlin live in salt water.

The marlin belongs to the sailfish family. Its dorsal fins are long and high, but not as high as those of the true sailfish. The ventral or pelvic fins are filamentous. The lower jaw is short. The upper jaw is prolonged into a round spear used as a club when catching fish. Their scales are thornlike.   J. C. K.

Marlin

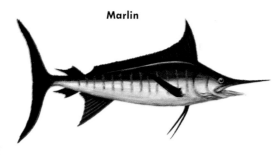

Marmoset (MAHR-muh-zett) Marmosets are a group of American monkeys. They are the smallest of all monkeys. When full grown they are about the size of squirrels or kittens. Their bodies are covered with long, soft, beautifully-colored fur that is striped on the tails.

Besides being smaller in size, marmosets differ in several ways from other American monkeys. They have thirty-two teeth rather than thirty-six. Their tails are not as useful to them, and they are unable to use their hands as skillfully as the other monkeys. Their toes have very sharp claws except for the large toe, which has a flat nail. G. A. D.
SEE ALSO: MONKEY, PRIMATE

Marmot Marmots include a number of rodents belonging to one group (genus *Marmota*) in the squirrel family. The woodchuck (also called *ground hog),* is about 2 feet (.61 meters) long and has yellowish brown fur with white on its snout. It weighs over 5 pounds (2.27 kilograms). It eats plant greens.

The *yellow-bellied marmot* lives in the western mountains of the United States where it is called the *rockchuck.* It is larger and heavier than the woodchuck. The *hoary marmot* also lives in the west. Its fur coat is silvery gray. When danger is approaching, it lets out a whistle-like sound.   H.J.C.

Marrow see Blood, Bone

Marmot

Mars Mars is one of the nine planets of the solar system. It is one of the four inner planets, and is the fourth planet from the sun. The orbit of Mars is larger than that of Earth, since it is about 50 million miles (80 million kilometers) farther from the sun. Mars' average distance from the sun is 142 million miles (229 million kilometers). Its diameter is 4,215 miles (6,783 kilometers), its period of revolution (year) is 687 days, and it has two satellite moons. In all probability, Mars is most like the Earth of all of the planets.

Mars does have an atmosphere; however, since Mars is much smaller than the earth, its surface gravity is only 38% of the Earth's. With such a low force of gravity, Mars cannot hold a very dense atmosphere. The Martian surface air pressure is much less than the Earth's. Its very thin atmosphere and scarcity of water vapor rule out the possibility of large amounts of liquid water on the surface. Perhaps in some locations water may exist for short periods during the summer or even possibly underground. Mars has polar ice caps, which contain both water ice and frozen carbon dioxide. They vary in size with the changing seasons.

Mars is reddish in color and has definite surface features, which were recognized and speculated about as early as the mid-seventeenth century. Study of these features has enabled astronomers to measure with precision the period of axial rotation of Mars as 24 hours, 37 minutes, and 22.7 seconds, only a little longer than that of Earth. These markings on the surface of Mars consist of dark areas (termed seas) and light areas (termed deserts) in a permanent pattern. The hue of Mars appears to change from its "summer" season to its "winter" season. In its summer season the planet appears to have somewhat of a greenish cast while the

NASA

winter exhibits more of a reddish hue. Most scientists attribute this to seasonal winds blowing dust. Occasionally, planet-wide dust storms can keep dust in the upper atmosphere for several weeks before it settles onto the surface. Based on both Mariner 9 and Viking spacecraft photographs, there is very good evidence to support this theory.

SPATIAL RELATIONSHIPS

Mars rotates on its axis every twenty-four hours, thirty-seven minutes and twenty-two and seven-tenths seconds. This is called its *sidereal day*—its day in relation to the stars in the heavens. It revolves around the sun in an elliptical path and requires 686.98 days to complete its orbit. This would take about one year and ten and one-half months of Earth's time. Since Earth revolves around the sun in less time than Mars does, it overtakes Mars every 780 days. Mars is then said to be *at opposition*—opposite the sun's place in the sky and nearer to Earth than usual. At certain times, however, Mars is not only at opposition, but also in its *perihelion*—in the position at which it is nearest to the sun. Then, Earth is between Mars and the sun. This phenomenon is called *favorable opposition*. It occurs every fifteen to seventeen years. At that time, Mars may be as little as 35,000,000 miles (56,327,000 kilometers) from Earth. Favorable oppositions occur in late summer or early fall. At these times, Mars becomes the brightest of the star-like objects except for Venus.

Favorable oppositions create good opportunities for astronomers to study Mars "close at hand." The last favorable opposition in 1971 offered the unique opportunity to compare Earth-based observations to

A picture taken by Viking II on Mars' Utopian plain shows the true color of the planet. Dust particles suspended in the air give the scene its red tint.

those made by the Mariner 9 spacecraft that was in orbit around Mars at that time.

Mars, like Earth, has a bulge at its equator and a slight flattening at the poles. Mars is roughly divided in to two hemispheres: the northern, which has large volcanoes and desert regions; and the southern, which is heavily cratered like the Moon. A vast canyon system stretches across the equator for almost 3,105 miles (4,997 kilometers). It may have been formed by water, but wind is the more likely erosion agent.

Through a good telescope, Mars reveals a variety of colors and markings. Reddish brown areas cover about three-fourths of the Martian surface. These are vast dust, sand, and boulder-strewn expanses of desert. The soil found there consists mainly of iron oxide minerals and a form of CLAY. The remaining portion of Mars consists of the dark regions and the polar caps. The dark (gray-green) regions were once thought to be rich in plant life because of their apparent darkening of color which corresponds to the coming of the spring and summer seasons. Spacecraft observations have since proved this theory wrong. The apparent darkening of these regions is the result of seasonal winds blowing lighter colored dust off the darker bedrock material of the surface. It is probably a BASALT.

In 1887, an Italian astronomer wrote of the fine, straight lines that he called *canals.* There has been much speculation as to the possibility of these "canals" being man-made. Modern astronomers think that these so-called canals are dark patches lying in shallow valleys. Their dark coloration may be caused by primitive vegetation.

THE ATMOSPHERE

The polar regions of Mars are ice-covered like the Earth's. They are composed of both water ice and frozen carbon dioxide. The actual thickness of the polar caps is not known, but reasonable estimates suggest a several hundred meter depth. Spacecraft photographs have shown several polar features like those formed by GLACIERS on Earth. It has been suggested that the polar caps of Mars could form a fairly thick atmosphere if they completely melted.

Because of its weaker gravitational pull, Mars has not been able to hold a very dense atmosphere. The chemical composition of its atmosphere, as determined by spacecraft measurements, is carbon dioxide (95%), oxygen (0.3-0.4%), nitrogen (2-3%), and argon (1-2%).

MARTIAN SEASONS

The *average* temperature on Mars is from −40 to −22° F. (−40° to −30° C.), averaged over days and nights, winters and summers. At noon on a summer Martian day near the equator, the temperature may reach 70° F. (21.1° C.). But at night, with little atmosphere to blanket in the heat, the temperature would drop to −90° F. (−67.8° C.).

Mars' axis inclines to the plane of its orbit at an angle of about 24°. This places the southern hemisphere a bit nearer the sun during the summer. The southern hemisphere has shorter but warmer summers than the northern hemisphere. Because Mars revolves in a more elongated, elliptical (less circular) orbit than Earth, its seasons are more unequal than those of Earth. In the northern hemisphere of Mars, the duration of the seasons are: spring, 199 terrestrial (Earth) days; summer, 182 days; autumn, 146 days; and winter, 160 days.

MARS' TWO SATELLITES

Mars has two small satellites. They are so small and so near the planet that they were not discovered until the favorable opposition of 1877, when Schiaparelli was mapping the *canali.* At that time Asaph Hall, at the Naval Observatory, Washington, D.C., discovered them. Because Mars had already been named after the god of war, the satellites were named *Phobos* and *Deimos* (Fear and Panic), the mythical Grecian companions of the god of war.

Phobos is the inner satellite. It has a shape with the dimensions of 27x21x19 kilometers and averages only 5,850 miles (9,414.66 kilometers) from the center of the planet, or 3,750 miles (6,035.04 kilometers) from its surface. It rises in the west and sets in the east, moving in a direction opposite to that of Mars' rotation.

It revolves once every seven hours and thirty-nine minutes. Phobos rises and sets twice in each Martian day.

Deimos, the outer satellite, had a shape of approximately 15x12 kilometers. It is 14,600 miles (23,496 kilometers) from the center of Mars, and 12,500 miles (20,117 kilometers) from the surface. It circles rapidly around Mars, once every thirty hours and eighteen minutes, slightly longer than the planet's own rotation time. From the surface of Mars, Deimos would appear to be moving very slowly—so slowly that it would go through all of its phases twice before it passed from one horizon to the other and out of sight. This would take two and one-half days.

THE EXPLORATION OF MARS

From 1964 to 1975, the U.S. launched six unmanned probes to Mars. *Mariner 4* completed a "flyby" mission in 1965, taking a series of twenty-two blurry pictures, the first close-up look at Mars. Two more Mariner flybys took much sharper images in 1969. The first probe to orbit Mars, *Mariner 9,* photographed the entire Martian surface before ending transmission in October 1972. *Mariner 9* photographed enormous volcanic mountains on the planet's surface.

The *Viking 1* and *Viking 2* probes were launched in 1975, and both made soft landings on Mars in 1976. Experiments designed to determine whether Martian soil contained living organisms were inconclusive and hard to explain. Expected to work for only 90 days, *Viking 1* transmitted pictures and data for over six years. *Viking 2* operated for three and a half years. No other probes were sent to Mars for seventeen years.

On Sept. 25, 1992, a *Titan 3* rocket carried the Mars Observer craft toward an orbital rendezvous with Mars in 1993. In January 1993, the spider-like robot *Dante* practiced entering an Antarctic volcano on earth in preparation for future exploration on Mars. A NASA official noted that the bitter cold Antarctic temperatures would be much like a spring day on Mars.　　　　　　J.H./P.P.S.

SEE ALSO: EARTH, PLANET, SOLAR SYSTEM, SPACE TRAVEL, VIKING PROJECT

Marsh A marsh is a natural community rich in plant and animal life. It may be formed as a result of beaver dams, a river changing its course, or a glacier thousands of years ago. A fresh water marsh is a body of shallow water, often with a mud bottom. Salt marshes form along coastal waters.

The index plants of a fresh water marsh are cattails, rushes, and sedges. Other plants include water lilies, arrowhead, pickerel weed, duckweed, and plankton. The index animals are the muskrat and red-winged blackbird, for both use cattails for food and to build their home or nest. A wide variety of birds nest in marshes and have a diet of fish. Amphibians, reptiles, rodents, and mammals use a marsh as a drinking fountain and source of food.

The natural aging (succession) of a marsh follows this pattern if the annual rainfall is sufficient; it will eventually fill in to become a wet meadow, then a prairie, and finally shrubs and trees will take over. People often look upon these lovely communities as wastelands, mosquito-infested low waters. They have been dredged for marinas, used as landfills for trash, or drained for farming. Due to people's carelessness, many species are destroyed.

Only recently have people realized the significance of salt marshes, which are in danger of disappearing. Marshes take up nitrates and phosphates and release oxygen. This is highly important in keeping pollutants down in the water just off shore. An effort is now underway to create new marshes to replace those destroyed in the past.　　　　　　H.J.C.

SEE ALSO: SUCCESSION

Marsh gas see Methane

Pelvic structure and pouch of a marsupial; marsupial bones support the pouch
Chicago Natural History Museum

Marsupial (mahr-SOO-pee-uhl) Animals that carry their babies in pockets on their bellies are called marsupials. *Marsupium* really means "pouch" or "bag."

Included in this interesting group of animals are great gray kangaroos, wallabies, opossums, Tasmanian wolves, and KOALAS. At one time, these animals were found all over the world. Now, most of them live in AUSTRALIA and on nearby islands. A few species live in South America but none are found in Europe, Asia, or Africa. The only species in North America is the Virginia opossum.

Since all marsupials are mammals, the females nourish their young on milk. They differ from other mammals, since their young are born small and underdeveloped. The newborn kangaroo is less than an inch (2.54 centimeters) in length. The small hind legs are like buds, but the well developed front legs have claws.

After birth, the young scramble through the mother's hair and climb up to the pouch by clawing with their limbs. In the pouch, they each cling tightly to a nipple. After weaning, when they are able to obtain their own food, they cling to the fur on the mother's back and ride about for protection.

Not all female marsupials have pouches. The banded anteater, for example, carries its young on the bottom of its body.

Marsupials have adapted themselves to many ways of life. Most marsupials are land animals, but one species of opossum lives in water. Some are nocturnal, and feed at night, while others feed by day. Koalas and opossums climb trees. Tasmanian wolves are carnivorous. Koalas feed on leaves from the giant gum tree. Some marsupials, like the pouched mole, are rodent-like, gnawing animals with well-developed incisors; others, like the bandicoots, feed upon insects.   E. P. L.
SEE ALSO: MAMMALIA, WALLABY

Marten see Weasel

Martin These birds are a type of swallow and are the largest birds in that family. Males are all blue-black. All other swallows have white bellies.

Groups of martins nest together, often using special houses. Females incubate four or five white eggs for about two weeks. Both parents feed the young. Martins live entirely on a diet of insects. In late summer, after the young are raised, martins leave their houses or nests and roam the countryside. At night they roost in trees in large flocks.   J. C. K.

Maser Maser comes from the words: Microwave Amplification by Stimulated Emission of Radiation. A maser is a beam of electromagnetic radiation. It is similar to a radio microwave, but very directional and coherent.

The maser, which uses QUANTIUM mechanics, amplifies short radio waves with extreme fidelity. Some gases, liquids, and solids, after absorbing such radiant energy as light, emit this energy instantly when triggered. If the emitted coherent radiation is in the microwave region, it is a maser; if it is in the visible region, it is a laser. With masers, more stable, noise-free methods of communication are achieved. A timing device (atomic clock) made with a gas maser loses not more than one second in one hundred years.   M. B. C.
SEE ALSO: LASER, ELECTROMAGNETIC RADIATION

The opossum is a North American marsupial

Purple martin

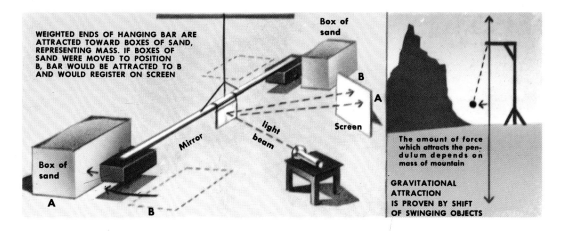

WEIGHTED ENDS OF HANGING BAR ARE ATTRACTED TOWARD BOXES OF SAND, REPRESENTING MASS. IF BOXES OF SAND WERE MOVED TO POSITION B, BAR WOULD BE ATTRACTED TO B AND WOULD REGISTER ON SCREEN

Box of sand

B
A

Screen

Mirror

light beam

Box of sand

A
B

Box of sand

The amount of force which attracts the pendulum depends on mass of mountain

GRAVITATIONAL ATTRACTION IS PROVEN BY SHIFT OF SWINGING OBJECTS

Mass Weight and mass are two different concepts often confused with each other. The WEIGHT of an object can change, depending on where it is. It will weigh less when at the equator or on a high mountain than it does when at the poles or on a low plain. But the mass of an object is the same anywhere it is placed.

An object in *free space*—far from the pull of gravity of other bodies—will have a definite mass but no weight.

Thus, mass measures the *actual* quantity of matter, while weight measures that quantity *indirectly* by its gravitational pull toward other objects.

Using Isaac Newton's Universal Law of Gravitation, Henry Cavendish (around 1800) calculated the mass of the earth. He used a simple but clever device, the TORSION balance. He supported a long rod from a quartz thread. The rod had lead balls on each end, and near each he fixed a larger lead ball. Measuring the sidewise twist caused by gravitational attraction between large and small balls, Cavendish calculated a value for "G," the gravitational constant, using Newton's formula:

$$F = \frac{G \, M_1 M_2}{d^2}$$

where M_1 is the mass of the small ball; M_2, that of the large; and d, the distance between. Then using the same formula, and knowing both the mass of an object at the surface of the earth and the earth's radius, Cavendish was able to calculate the mass of the earth.

CONSERVATION OF MASS

The *law of conservation of mass* states that in any ordinary chemical reaction, the mass of the reacting substance is exactly equal to the mass of the products. It was stated in 1756 by Lomonossov (Russian), and independently by LAVOISIER (French) in 1774. Landolt (German chemist) confirmed it by careful experiments from 1893 to 1908.

Note that the law says "ordinary chemical reactions," excluding nuclear reactions involving radioactive changes. EINSTEIN'S theory of mass-energy equivalence states that the mass plus the energy of the reactants in a reaction must equal the mass *plus* the energy of the products of the reaction. If the mass of the products is less than that of the starting materials, some of the original mass has been converted to energy. This is the process which releases energy when an atomic bomb explodes.

Robert Millikan (American) performed a famous "charged oil drop" experiment and measured the electric charge on electrons in 1916. J. J. Thomson (English) used Millikan's data to calculate an electron's mass, which he found to be 9.1072×10^{-31} kilograms.   E. Y. K.

SEE ALSO: FORCE, GRAVITY, MEASUREMENT, MILLIKAN'S ELECTRONIC CHARGE, RELATIVITY, WEIGHTLESSNESS

Mass defect see Nuclear science glossary

Mass number see Nuclear science glossary

Master gland see Endocrine gland, Pituitary

Chicago Natural History Museum
Mastodon

Mastodon (MASS-tuh-don) Mastodons were huge, shaggy-haired elephants that appeared on earth about 20 million years ago.

Mastodons became extinct only several thousand years ago. They lived at the same time as early man. The oldest types had tusked lower jaws 5 to 6 feet (1.5 to 1.8 meters) long. These were used to dig out roots. Later mastodons were larger. Their lower jaws shortened and their upper tusks developed. Upper tusks up to 11 feet (3.4 meters) long curved up. American fossil forms look like modern elephants, but have shorter legs and wider feet. Mastodons ate grass, branches, and leaves. Huge molars gave the beast its common name. J.C.K.

SEE ALSO: FOSSILS, MAMMOTH

Mastoid (MASS-toyd) The mastoid is a bony elevation located behind and a little below the ear. It is made up of bony air cells, and its triangular shape makes it project prominently. In early life there may be only one air cell; but as a person grows older, more cells develop and the mastoid becomes more prominent.

These cells, similar to hollowed out areas in the bone, communicate with the cavity of the middle ear. It is this easy communication between the mastoid cells and the cavity of the ear which may lead to trouble when INFECTION develops after an earache. H. K. S.

Matches Matches have been known since 1781, but the earliest types were generally inconvenient, and expensive. Too often they were made of poisonous materials or gave off poisonous gases. Today's matches are easy to use, work well under most conditions,

STRIKE ANYWHERE—PHOSPHORUS AND ABRASIVE

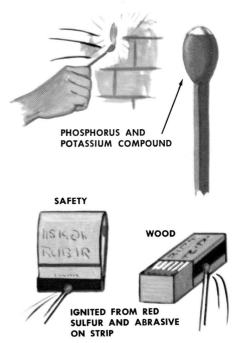

PHOSPHORUS AND POTASSIUM COMPOUND

SAFETY

WOOD

IGNITED FROM RED SULFUR AND ABRASIVE ON STRIP

Strike-anywhere matches and safety matches differ in the placement of ignition material

and are cheap and safe to use where reasonable safety is practiced. Caution in use and storage of matches can prevent many serious fires. The commonest varieties of matches are strike-anywhere matches and safety matches.

Strike-anywhere matches are made of wood splints, treated against after-glow, and paraffined for better burning. The head is made of two parts, the white tip or eye, and the red, blue, or black bulbous base. The eye is made of a PHOSPHORUS compound which ignites at a relatively low temperature, created by the friction from striking it. The fire ignites the base, which cannot ignite itself. It provides heat sufficient to light the paraffin coating and subsequently the wood.

Safety matches, packed in books or boxes, divide the ignition material between the match head and package. Thus they cannot light except by friction with a special striking surface. The head is a POTASH compound, while the striking surface is made of red phosphorus and sand.

The United States leads in production of both types of matches. D. J. I.

Mathematics Mathematics has been called "the queen of knowledge." A most important fact about the real, material world is that objects in it can be counted and their masses can be measured. Mathematics is a tool which helps man know how much, how many, how large, how fast, in what direction, and with what chances. But mathematics is more than just a system of numbers (*numeration*). It is also a way of thinking and a form of logical reasoning. From this manner of reasoning about numbers and space, ideas and conclusions can be developed.

Mathematics grew up with civilization as man's quantitative needs increased. It arose out of practical problems and man's need to solve these problems. As soon as man began to count, even on his fingers, mathematics began. It was the first of the sciences to develop formally. It is growing faster today than in its early beginnings. New questions are always arising, partly from practical problems and partly from pure, theoretical problems. In each generation, men have developed new methods and ideas to solve these problems. While thousands of great mathematicians have shared in this work, some feel that the greatest were ARCHIMEDES, ISAAC NEWTON, and Carl Friedrich Gauss.

The Greeks elevated mathematics to the field of abstract thinking. In its higher form mathematics becomes a form of logic in which basic assumptions are laid down and results are then deduced within the framework of the system. The system, itself, is composed of (1) a few, elementary, undefined terms, such as number, point, and line, which are called *primitives;* and (2) rules which govern their operations. The primitives comprise the basic vocabulary of mathe-

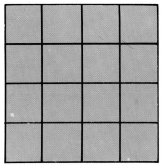

Example of a mathematics puzzle: using the numbers 1 through 16 only once, arrange them so that the sum of the columns, rows, and diagonals is 34 (answer on page 1030)

matics and provide the groundwork for a more technical vocabulary within the system. The basic definitions are stated in terms of the primitives, as are the *postulates,* which are assumptions or evident truths. With these tools, then, statements and conclusions can be derived or proved. The results, in turn, assist in proving more statements. Thus, a large structure is built.

However, mathematics is much more than just a system of conclusions drawn from definitions and postulates that must be consistent. Even though the assumptions may be created by the free will of the mathematician, there must be a very strong relationship of the abstract mathematical principle to its physical counterpart in the real, material world. Otherwise, mathematics would be only an intellectual pastime or game without any real purpose. Only after extensive calculations, tests, and observations are the assumptions admitted to the system.

In their determination to have mathematical principles correspond to events in the real world, mathematicians went too far in considering certain objects, such as numbers, points, lines, etc. as substantial things in themselves. Since these concepts had never really been carefully defined–only "discussed," it finally occurred to the mathematicians of the nineteenth century that there was no necessity of attaching a meaning to these objects as real, physical things. The mathematical principles involving these objects do not refer to their tangible reality. The principles state only the interrelations between the objects and the rules governing operations with them. In other words, what points, lines, and numbers actually are cannot and need not be discussed.

While mathematics originated from phys-

Seven men each have seven sacks. In each sack are seven cats. Each of the cats has seven kittens. How many legs are there in the group?

Answer: 7 men with 7 sacks = 49 sacks
1 sack has 7 cats + 49 kittens = 56 animals
56 animals with 4 legs each = 224 cat legs
224 cat legs × 49 sacks = 10,976 cat legs
7 men with 2 legs = 14 legs
10,976 cat legs + 14 people legs = 10,990 legs!

ONE OF MANY
POSSIBLE SOLUTIONS
TO THE PUZZLE
ON PAGE 1029

2	11	13	8
16	5	3	10
7	14	12	1
9	4	6	15

ical situations, such as primitive man's counting the animals he killed on one day, real progress in this science began only after the concrete pictures, emotions, and physical concepts were isolated from the numbers themselves. This isolation or abstraction of numbers actually simplified mathematics since the distractions and confusion of images were gone. At this time emerged *pure* mathematics—the science of number and quantity unconnected with any material object. *Arithmetic, algebra, geometry, trigonometry,* and the more advanced branches of mathematics can each be considered as pure mathematics only if the concepts attach no real, tangible application.

Mathematics in the service of the physical sciences—such as mechanics, engineering, optics, astronomy, geodesy and electricity—is referred to as *applied mathematics.* The applied mathematician takes the pure mathematician's findings and applies them to the varied concrete situations. After pure mathematics emerged from primitive man's applied mathematics, the pure was then reapplied. As this pattern was repeated throughout history, the science developed. However, this pattern is not the only sequence of development nor even the best one for scientific discovery.

Mathematics is characterized by its own symbolic language. This is a great aid for pure mathematicians in their attempt to strip all concreteness from the field, but it also helps all mathematicians. By eliminating the cumbersome consequences of everyday language, such as the interpretations and misinterpretations, ambiguity and lack of precision of many words and phrases, the science has been developed greatly. The carefully designed compactness of the symbols make for clarity of thought. The preciseness of its language aims at brevity—essential for exact thinking. The language is universal. Mathematicians of all countries use the unique symbols of mathematics.

No one has yet been able to give one completely comprehensive answer to the question, "what is mathematics?" One reason is that it is a growing and changing body of knowledge, rich in ideas and varied in the aspects it covers. Mathematics may be considered a method—a way of examining problems and of reasoning. Mathematics may be considered an art—a human creation. Mathematics may be considered a language—a way to communicate about quantity, time, and space. It is a body of knowledge serving the physical and social scientist, the philosopher, the logician, and the artist. In spite of its assumption-based nature, mathematics has given humans the tools with which to describe nature. Although modern science has achieved much by virtue of mathematics, the two fields are distinct. Mathematics has contributed to the development of the sciences, and by assisting rational thought it also has contributed greatly to the development of civilization. D.L.D./M.M.L.

SEE ALSO: ALGEBRA, ARITHMETIC, GEOMETRY

Matter Matter is generally defined as anything which has weight and occupies space. All matter is composed of units called *molecules* and *atoms*. These atoms also have weight and occupy space. Basically, ATOMS are made of electrically-charged particles —*protons,* found in the nucleus, and *electrons,* traveling about the nucleus. In addition, there are *neutrons* in the nucleus with a weight similar to protons, but lacking charge. Hydrogen is the only element which, in simple form, has no neutrons in the nucleus.

In the solid state, atoms vibrate closely but cannot move around one another

The relations of matter to ENERGY are explored by physical scientists. Large pieces of matter, when moving, have mechanical energy. Streams of electrons from atoms carry electrical energy. Chemical changes either set free or store up energy as new groups of atoms (molecules) are formed. Some atoms such as uranium and radium automatically break down, letting loose certain particles along with freed energy from their nuclei.

In the liquid state, packing is slightly less and atoms slide past others

Matter exists in different stages, such as solids, liquids, gases, and plasmas. Each has a different set of physical properties, depending on how much heat energy the matter contains. For example, if heat energy is added to ice, it melts. This energy gives the molecules of water greater freedom of motion than the ice molecules had. Heat added to water at the boiling point changes water to a gas (water vapor). Still more heat would tear the electrons away from the oxygen and hydrogen, producing ionic plasma. More heat would produce nuclear plasma.

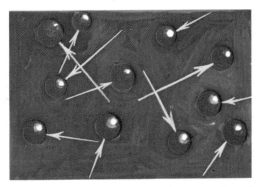

In the gaseous state, atoms bounce off and move one another

Matter is classified as *organic* and *inorganic.* Often organic matter is defined as that which is living or once lived. Another basis is the presence of carbon in organic matter, versus its absence in inorganic.

Matter is measured in terms of weight or MASS. Mass is preferable as it refers to the actual quantity of a given material. WEIGHT is a measure of gravitational attraction. This varies with the location of the bodies involved. Because of gravity a pound (kilogram) of butter "weighs" more on Earth than on the moon; yet its mass remains constant.

Matter has chemical properties, peculiarities of behavior with other kinds of matter. Wood burns, forming new products. This represents chemical change. Both groups of properties are used in classifying matter.

The "Law of Conservation of Energy" states that "matter cannot be created or destroyed." This is amended with " . . . by ordinary means." Another version states that there exists a given amount of ENERGY and matter, known to be interchangeable. D. J. I.
SEE ALSO: ANTIMATTER, ATOM, CHEMICAL CHANGE, CHEMISTRY, NUCLEAR SCIENCE, ORGANIC COMPOUNDS, PHYSICAL STATES AND CHANGES

May apple see Wild flowers

May fly The May fly is a slender insect with large front wings and small back wings. It may live for years in its aquatic larval stage, but only a few days in the adult stage.

Mayer, Maria (1906-1972) In 1963, Ms. Mayer shared the NOBEL PRIZE in physics with Hans Jensen for her work in nuclear-shell theory. Her career involved both nuclear physics and statistical mechanics. She did important work on the theory of the atomic *nucleus*.   A.J.H.

Meadowlark The common meadowlark belongs to the blackbird family. They have brown backs and wings, white feathers on the sides of short tails, and yellow breasts marked with a black V. Their heads are striped with tan. A meadowlark's song is a musical, slurred whistle. They feed chiefly on insects.

Meadowlarks have a distinctive flight. They alternate rapid short wingbeats with periods of soaring. They live in open meadows or fields, as their name implies.

Meadowlarks are ground birds that walk rather than hop. Their grass nests, while placed on the ground, are cleverly concealed. A shallow depression is lined with pine needles, horsehair, or other materals. The female weaves a covering of growing grass over the top of the nest. She lays about five white eggs blotched with lavender and brown. Only the female incubates the eggs, leaving them for short periods while she feeds. J. C. K.

Eastern meadowlark

Mealworm Mealworms are the young or larvae of a small beetle called a *darkling beetle*. They live in cereals and are common in places where cereals are stored, such as grocery stores. Mealworms are sold in pet stores as food for pet toads, lizards, frogs, and birds.

Mealworms for pet food can be raised at home. A heavy cardboard container partly filled with oatmeal and covered with cloth serves the purpose. Larvae purchased from the store will go into a resting stage in the meal. They emerge as adult, slender, black beetles. If the larvae are to be used as pet food, they should be kept in meal in a screw top jar in the refrigerator.   B. J. C.
SEE ALSO: BEETLE, LARVA

Measles Measles (also called rubeola or "red measles") is an acute, highly contagious disease. Its symptoms are a fever and spotting on the skin. It usually affects children. Adults can contract the disease if they have never had it in childhood. One attack usually protects the individual from future attacks, but there are similar diseases, such as *German measles,* from which the patient is not protected.

After a person has been exposed, a period of ten days or two weeks elapses before the patient shows any signs of illness. The illness starts in a mild way with a chill, a slight fever, a "running" nose, a cough, and reddened eyes. After three or four days a dusky red rash breaks out on the skin and even shows itself on the inside of the mouth. The rash and other symptoms continue for about four days and gradually subside. The skin clears as the patient recovers.

The disease is caused by a VIRUS which is passed from one person to another in the early stages of the illness. Measles once was thought to be a mild disease, but it is now considered serious and sometimes fatal if it is complicated by PNEUMONIA or ENCEPHALITIS. Even mild cases lower resistance, making the patient more susceptible for a time to tuberculosis and other bacterial illnesses. Now that there is a VACCINATION for measles, it could be almost completely eradicated. Children need only one "shot" at 15 months of age.   H.K.S./E.S.S.

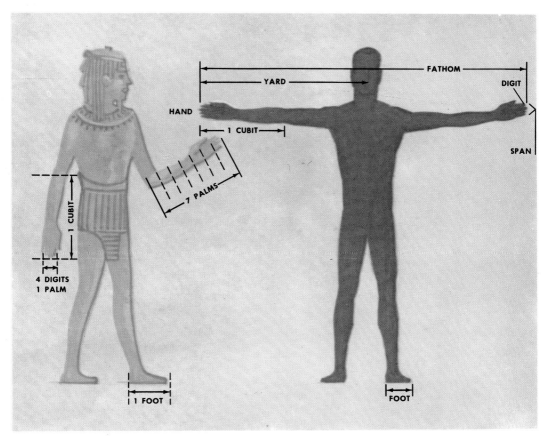

Man has used many devices to measure things. He also has devised different systems for describing measurement as he discovered a need for them

Measurement Things are measured in order to find out their size. The most convenient measure to use depends upon the size of the object being measured. Lengths can be measured in inches (centimeters), in feet (meters), in yards (meters), or even in miles (kilometers). Force can be measured in ounces (grams), in pounds (kilograms), or in tons (metric *tons*). Time can be measured in seconds, in minutes, in hours, in years, or in centuries. Temperature is measured in degrees. Angles are subdivided into degrees, minutes, and seconds.

A measurement always results in a number and a unit of measure; for example, 3 feet (0.91 meter), 15 seconds, 8 pounds (3.63 kilograms). The number tells how many units are needed to equal the units in the thing being measured. The unit of measure tells what standard unit has been used, such as the inch (centimeter), foot (meter), ton (metric *ton*), or degree. The United States government has set the value of each common unit to ensure that all measurements are in standard units over the entire country. The United States uses primarily the British (imperial) system, while most other countries use the METRIC SYSTEM of measurement.

The origin of the basic units of measurements, and their subdivisions and multiples, can be traced to many ancient civilizations. The Chinese and Egyptians divided units into tenths. The Romans subdivided into twelfths—twelve inches in a foot;

MEASUREMENT OF SIZE

Linear (length or width)

12 inches (in.)	1 foot (ft.)
3 feet	1 yard (yd.), 36 in.
5½ yards	1 rod (rd.), 16½ ft.
40 rods	1 furlong (fur.), 220 yds.; 660 ft.
8 furlongs	1 statute mile (mi.), 1760 yds.
3 miles	1 league (l.), 5280 yds.

Square (area) (length and width)

144 square inches (sq. in.)	1 sq. ft.
9 sq. ft.	1 sq. yd.; 1296 sq. in.
30¼ sq. yd.	1 sq. rod; 272¼ sq. ft.
160 sq. rods.	1 acre (A.); 4840 sq. yds.
640 acres	1 sq. mile; 3097 sq. yds.
36 sq. miles	1 township

Cubic (length, width, height)

1728 cubic inches (cu. in.)	1 cu. ft.
27 cu. ft.	1 cu. yd.
144 cu. in.	1 board foot
128 cu. ft.	1 cord

MEASUREMENT OF WEIGHT

Avoirdupois (all commodities except precious stones, metals, drugs)

27¹¹⁄₃₂ grain (gr.)	1 dram (dr.)
16 drams	1 ounce (oz.); 437½ grains
16 ounces	1 pound (lb.); 256 drams; 7000 grains
100 pounds	1 hundredweight (cwt); 1600 oz.
112 pounds	1 long hundredweight (l. cwt)
20 hundredweight.	1 ton (tn.); 2000 pounds
20 long hundredweight. .	1 long ton (l. tn.); 2240 pounds

Troy (money, jewels, precious stones)

20 mites	1 grain
3.086 grains	1 carat
24 grains (gr.)	1 pennyweight (dwt)
20 pennyweights	1 ounce (oz.t.); 480 grains
12 ounces	1 pound (lb.t.); 240 pennyweights

Apothecary (dry) drugs

20 grains (gr.)	1 scruple
3 scruples	1 dram
8 drams	1 ounce; 24 scruples; 480 grains
12 ounces.	1 pound

(fluid)

60 minims.	1 fluid dram
8 fluid drams.	1 fluid ounce
16 fluid ounces	1 pint
8 pints.	1 gallon

UNITS OF WAVE MOTION

Cycle—One complete movement of a wave
Frequency—The number of cycles or complete waves in one second
Wave length—The distance of a cycle, measured in the direction of the wave in Angstrom units (see light)
Decibel—A measure of the loudness of sound

MEASUREMENT OF CAPACITY

Liquid

4 gills . . . . . . (liquids)	1 pint
2 pints.	1 quart
4 quarts	1 gallon; 8 pints
31½ gallons.	1 barrel
2 barrels.	1 hogshead

Dry

2 pints (pt.) . . . . (dry measure)	1 quart
8 quarts	1 peck
4 pecks.	1 bushel
105 quarts	1 barrel

ELECTRICAL UNITS

Ampere—Unit for constant flow of electric current
Ohm—Unit for resistance to flow
Volt—Unit of electromotive force. One volt is the amount of electrical force necessary to drive one ampere through a resistance of one ohm
Coulomb—Unit of charge. One coulomb is transported by one ampere in one second
Farad—Unit of capacity. One farad will hold one coulomb where a difference of potential of one volt exists
Henry—Unit of inductance. The inductance of a closed circuit in which an electromotive force of one volt is produced when the electric current in the circuit varies uniformly at a rate of one ampere per second
Weber—Unit of magnetic flux, linking a circuit of one turn, produces in it an electromotive force of one volt as it is reduced at a uniform rate in one second

MECHANICAL UNITS

Derived from metric system:

Dyne—Unit of force, which acting on one gram produces an acceleration of one centimeter per second per second
Newton—Unit of force which gives to a mass of the kilogram an acceleration of one meter per second per second
Joule—Unit of energy or work done when the point of application of the newton is displaced a distance of one meter in the direction of the force
Watt—Unit of power which gives rise to the production of energy at the rate of one joule per second
Bar—Unit of pressure or one million dynes acting on one square centimeter

Derived from imperial system:

Foot-pound—Unit of energy or the work done when one pound is raised one foot
Horse-power—Unit of power. One H.P. is the energy required to lift 550 pounds one foot in one second
Tensile strength—Unit of strain. The number of pounds of pressure a material can bear without breaking. Measured in pounds per square inch
Poundal—Unit of force which, when acting on a weight of one pound, produces an acceleration of one foot per second per second

TIME UNITS

60 seconds	1 minute
60 minutes	1 hour
24 hours	1 day
7 days	1 week
14 days	1 fortnight
29½ days	1 lunar month
365 days, 5 hours, 48 minutes, 7 sec.	1 year
10 years	1 decade
100 years	1 century
1000 years	1 millenium

ASTRONOMICAL UNITS

The astronomical unit—Distance from earth to sun
—149,501,201 kilometers
— 92,900,000 miles
The light second— 299,790 kilometers
The light-year—9.4614×10^{15} meters, which is approximately 6,000,000,000,000 miles
The parsec—the distance at which the annual parallax of a star would be 1 inch.
—3.258 light-years
—3.0838×10^{16} meters

CIRCULAR MEASUREMENT

Circular measurement:

60 seconds (″)	1 minute (′)
60 minutes	1 degree (°)
90 degrees	1 quadrant (quad)
4 quadrants	1 circle

NAUTICAL MEASURE

Nautical measure:

6 feet	1 fathom
100 fathoms	1 cable's length (ordinary)
120 fathoms	1 cable's length (United States Navy)
10 cables' lengths	1 nautical mile
1 nautical mile	1.1515 statute mile, 1 minute
60 nautical miles	1 degree

LIGHT UNITS

Angstrom (Å)—Unit of length, measures wave length. One Angstrom is 1/250 millionth of an inch or 1/100 millionth centimeter

Candle power—Unit for the standard measurement of light. It is the light given off by the flame of a candle of definite size, shape, type of tallow, and wick (the standard candle)

Foot candle—Unit of brightness on a surface one foot away from a light of one candle power

Lumen—Unit of measurement for the amount of light falling on a surface from an intensity of one candle

MISCELLANEOUS OTHER UNITS

c.m.u. (chemical mass unit)—Unit of chemical atomic weight
m.u. (physical mass unit)—Unit of physical mass based on the atomic weight of oxygen taken as exactly 16.1 m.u. = atomic weight of oxygen
e—The charge of the electron. The smallest known natural unit of electricity
Curie—A unit for the rate of disintegration of a radioactive substance
Rutherford (rd)—A unit for the rate of disintegration of a radioactive substance. 1 rd. is the amount of radioactive substance which undergoes ten million disintegrations per second
Roentgen—A unit of gamma or X-ray radiation

HEAT UNITS

Calorie—Metric unit of heat energy. The quantity of heat needed to warm one gram of water one degree C. (cal.)

Large Calorie—1000 calories. Used in biology as the measure of the fuel value of food. If bread contains 100 large calories, it can supply the body with enough heat to raise 1000 grams of water 100° C. (Cal.)

B.T.U.—Imperial unit of heat. The quantity of heat required to raise the temperature of one pound of water through one ° F. 1 B.T.U. = 252 calories

CONVERSION TABLE

Metric system into imperial system

centimeter	0.3937	inch
meter	39.37	inches (exactly)
square centimeter	.1549997	square inch
square meter	1.195985	square yards
hectare	2.47104	acres
cubic meter	1.3079428	cubic yards
liter	.264178	gallon
liter	1.05671	liquid quarts
liter	.908102	dry quart
hectoliter	2.83782	bushels
gram	15.432356	grains
kilogram	2.204622341	pounds, avoirdupois

Imperial system into metric system

inch	2.54005	centimeters
foot	30.4806	centimeters
yard	.9144018	meter
square inch	6.451626	sq. centimeters
square yard	.8361307	sq. meter
acre	.404687	hectare
cubic yard	.7645594	cubic meter
gallon	3.785332	liters
liquid quart	.946333	liter
dry quart	1.101198	liters
bushel	35.23833	liters
grain	.064798918	gram
pound, avoirdupois	.4535924277	kilogram

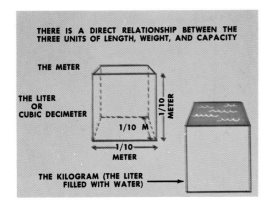

THERE IS A DIRECT RELATIONSHIP BETWEEN THE THREE UNITS OF LENGTH, WEIGHT, AND CAPACITY

THE METER

THE LITER OR CUBIC DECIMETER

1/10 M

1/10 METER

1/10 METER

THE KILOGRAM (THE LITER FILLED WITH WATER)

twelve months in a year. The Hindus divided into halves, quarters, eighths, and sixteenths. The ancient Babylonians used sixty divisions.

Throughout the centuries many different units have been used. Some of these units are the perch, barleycorn, noggin, gill, tuffet, pottle, jack, jill, jock, joey, scruple, and hogshead. Some of these units are still used for special measurements. Look at the tables on pages 1034 and 1035 and see which of these units are still used.

Although many different units of measurement have been used, the process of measurement has remained essentially the same. For example, to measure length one chooses a unit of length and compares the length being measured to this unit. If the length is longer than the unit, then one finds how many of these units are needed to make a length as long. If the length is shorter then one finds what proportion it is of the unit.

To help one count the units when measuring there is often an instrument. A ruler will show how many units (such as centimeters or inches) long an object is. A scale will show how many units an object weighs. A thermometer tells how many degrees of temperature are present. The clock even counts—it counts the units of duration.

The basic quantities that are measured are length, mass, time, and temperature. It is possible to express many other measurable things in terms of these quantities. Area is expressed in terms of length. The area of a rectangle is the length times the width. Volume is expressed in terms of cubic units of length. Speed is the distance traveled divided by the time in motion (length ÷ time). A calorie is the quantity of heat needed to warm one gram of water one degree Celsius.

STANDARDS

The basic units of measurement—the meter, kilogram, liter—have been standardized by international agreement. The standard units, called the *international prototypes,* are kept near Paris at the International Bureau of Weights and Measures. The standard meter, constructed in 1889, is the distance between two hair lines on a bar of platinum-iridium when the bar is at a temperature of 0° C. A more precise measurement defines the meter in terms of the wave length of red cadmium light waves under specified conditions of temperature, pressure, and humidity. One meter is 1,553,164.13 of these red cadmium wave lengths.

The standard kilogram is a cylinder of platinum-iridium, the length of which is approximately equal to its diameter. The liter is a secondary unit and is defined as the volume of a kilogram of pure water at specific temperature and pressure. One liter = 1000.028 cc. Copies of the international prototypes have been constructed by different nations so that comparisons to the standard can easily be made. In the United States the National Bureau of Standards is part of the Department of Commerce. Here copies of the standard meter and kilogram are kept, and industrial standards of length and mass are often compared to make sure that they are accurate.

A machine called a *comparator* can compare lengths to a few millionths of an inch. Delicate balances compare weights so that a difference of one part in 100 million can be detected. True measurement can never be exact but involves the statement of two limits. The difference between these two limits is dependent on the measuring instrument. A micrometer is more accurate than a yardstick; a mass spectrometer is more accurate than a micrometer. The National Bureau of Standards constantly strives to develop more precise measuring instruments and more exact ways of measuring. It serves both science and industry as a research center and a testing and checking bureau. H. W. M.

SEE ALSO: CALENDAR; CALIPER; CLOCKS; COLOR; DAY AND NIGHT; EARTH; EQUINOX; INTERNATIONAL DATE LINE; MATHEMATICS; MOON, PHASES OF; NAVIGATION; TEMPERATURE SCALES; TIME ZONES

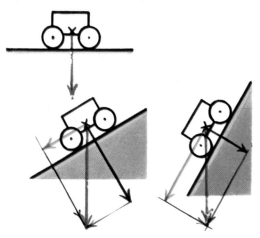

A greater force would be needed on a steeper incline to overcome the component of gravity and move the car upward

Mechanical advantage A claw hammer gives you a mechanical advantage when you pull out a nail. Force must be used on the nail to pull it from the board. The hammer requires a smaller force at the handle to produce the large force at the nail.

Mechanical advantage is defined as the quotient of the force produced by the device and the force exerted on the device. In the example of the hammer and nail, the mechanical advantage would be calculated as follows:

$$\text{M.A.} = \frac{\text{Force exerted on nail}}{\text{Force exerted on hammer handle}}$$

The preceding example shows the hammer to be a kind of lever. The fulcrum is the place where the hammer contacts the board. Friction at the fulcrum is not considered here. Other devices which have a mechanical advantage are: pulleys and belts (or ropes in the case of a block and tackle); gears; hydraulic and pneumatic cylinders; cams; and the inclined plane, of which the screw thread is an example.   M. W. K.

SEE ALSO: MACHINERY; MACHINES, SIMPLE

Mechanics Mechanics is the science which deals with the effect of forces upon matter at rest or matter in motion. The laws of solids, liquids, and gases have a part in this process. Mechanics is one of the basic studies of ENGINEERING, PHYSICS, and ASTRONOMY.

Mechanics deals with forces and the motion produced by them. People often think of a force as a push or a pull, but the idea of force as that which produces or destroys motion is modern. This concept of force has been useful, and can be attributed to ISAAC NEWTON, who is considered the chief founder of the science of mechanics.

The ancients knew little about mechanics, and what they did know was about non-moving mechanics or *statics*. The Greek ARCHIMEDES was familiar with the principles of the lever and pulley and their relationships. In the fifteenth century LEONARDO DA VINCI generalized the principle of the inclined plane and the composition of forces. Varignon expounded the principle of moments and also the composition of forces. GALILEO, in studying the inclined plane, discovered the principle of virtual work. BERNOULLI made general Galileo's concepts of virtual work. These are the chief names in the development of statics.

Most important of all was the work of Isaac Newton, who not only made universal the ideas of force and introduced the notion of mass, but laid down exact definitions and principles of mechanics that stand today.

The portion of mechanics that deals with forces in EQUILIBRIUM is known by the term *statics,* which means standing still. Contrasted with this is *dynamics,* which deals with the effects of forces that act to produce motion in bodies. Since motion is seen in all matter, the laws of motion involve the basic properties of matter.

Kinematics is the mathematical description of the motions of moving objects as a function of time. For example, the kinematic description of a rock being whirled around at the end of a string would be given by writing down the circumference of a circle. This would give the position of the rock at each instant of time. Another kinematic equation would tell how fast the rock was moving. But the kinematic equations would say nothing about the forces exerted on the string by the rock, or the forces on the hand by the string. The study of the forces producing motion, or the forces caused by motion, is called *dynamics.*

Aerospace scientists use mechanics to design planes and satellites. Architects and engineers constantly use its laws to figure the correct bending and twisting forces in new buildings and machines. Figuring sizes and motions of stars and planets is based on mechanics. Even nuclear and molecular physicists start from the laws of mechanics to derive predictions about how the basic particles of matter will behave.

Hydrostatics and *hydraulics* deal with fluids at rest and in motion. AERODYNAMICS is the study of air or other gases as they move past solid objects.   V. V. N.
SEE ALSO: DYNAMICS, FORCES, STRESS

Medawar, Peter B. (1915-1988) Peter Medawar was a co-winner of the 1960 NOBEL PRIZE in physiology or medicine for his experiments in the field of immunology.

Medawar studied the causes for the rejection of skin grafts. The results of his experiments with laboratory animals could have important applications to the treatment of humans with organ transplants. During World War II, Medawar prepared a substance known as *fibrinogen*. It became important in the treatment of burn victims requiring skin grafts.

Medawar and FRANK MACFARLANE BURNET were awarded the Nobel Prize for their work on the concept of *tolerance*. By injecting unborn mice with cells from a donor, they proved that the mice demonstrated an acquired immunological tolerance for the donor's tissues after birth. The theory is not yet applicable to humans.   A.J.H.

Median (MEE-dee-un) Median means "middle." The median of a body or figure is the line that divides the body or figure lengthwise into equal halves. In a series of numbers such as 1 3 4 7 9, the median is the middle number —in this case it would be four. In an even series of numbers, the median is halfway between the two middle ones.
SEE: STATISTICS

Medicinal plants see Economic botany; Herb; Plants, medicinal

Medicine The general term *medicine* refers to the art and science of healing the sick. It includes the prevention of sickness and community sanitation and hygiene. As a career, medicine deserves the most careful consideration by the young student. It offers a very real opportunity to serve fellow human beings in a concrete and helpful way. It stimulates a desire for an ever broader knowledge of the arts, the sciences, the cultures, and the traditions of the human race.

HISTORY

The history of medicine goes back to earliest recorded knowledge. It has developed from these early times to the present period of greater accomplishment along with the advance of all sciences.

After studying the medicine man of ancient tribal life and his struggle to understand the cause of disease, the medical student may study medicine as practiced in dawning civilizations. Tracing Babylonian culture from its established records between 6000 and 7000 years ago, he will find the men of medicine were highly respected in that society. These early physicians recognized a power to heal greater than themselves and were referred to as servants of the various gods then worshipped. In medicine there were gods who helped mothers in childbirth, others who helped those wounded in battle. Hammurabi, who lived about 2200 B.C. provided a fee schedule for physicians in his legal code. This alone testifies that medical activity was thought of as a profession at that time.

About the time these developments were taking place in Mesopotamia, medicine was

Medicine

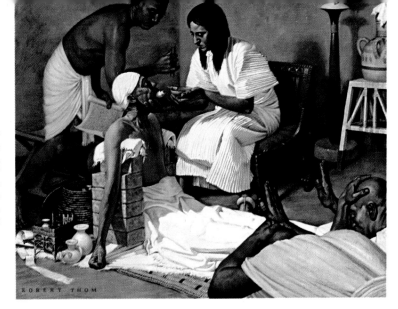

In ancient Egypt (about 1500-1400 B.C.) physicians were viewed with respect. They knew the value of cleanliness. However, much of their work was done with the religious priests, preventing medicine from becoming more scientific

also recognized as a respected profession in Egypt. This Egyptian activity, however, did not contribute as much toward present day medicine. Egyptians were essentially mystic and seemed inclined to attach a priestly function to medicine. Less is known about Egyptian medicine because records were not as well-preserved. One factor probably responsible was the practice of using papyrus on which to write their medical theses. PAPYRUS is a very fragile substance which does not withstand the ravages of time as well as parchment, tablets made of clay or sheepskin.

As Greece developed, she made her medical superiority felt in both Egypt and Mesopotamia. Greece acquired and developed medical lore from the contributions of all the peoples inhabiting the shores of the Mediterranean. Only in Greece were there men and groups dedicated to the search for more knowledge free of the chains imposed by cults. Greek physicians absorbed the treasures of all the arts and sciences, of philosophy, astronomy, and mathematics, unhindered by prejudice.

It was Greece that developed a systematic body of thought for practicing medicine. Its physicians followed an organized method of training and in consequence were accorded the respect of the world. In Homer's poems one learns that practitioners of medicine ranked with musicians, philosophers and architects. True, medicine had its gods such as Apollo, Aesculapius and his daughter, Hygieie, but these deities were outside of medicine. The temples dedicated to them served as places of rest for the sick. By the time of HIPPOCRATES (460 B.C.), Greek physicians were quite ready to deny that DIS-EASE was of supernatural origin. They had slowly gotten rid of magic concepts and dogmatic priestly ideas were less in evidence. Medicine was establishing a firmer understanding based on observation of the sick and a biologic study of man and animals.

Thus was born a broader understanding of man and his relationship to nature. This spirit, dedicated to the acquisition of knowledge, was prevalent all through Greece and its colonies, Alexandria and the islands. In fact, one of the islands became quite famous as a mecca of healing—the island of Cos which was the birthplace of Hippocrates. Hippocrates came to dominate the schools of medicine of his time and was a leader among physicians. He used a knowledge of the past to develop a system of healing acknowledging that nature was the healing force and that the chief function of the physician was to aid nature.

This more rational type of medicine entered the Roman civilization with the subjection of the Greeks and the expulsion of the more learned from Alexandria. The Romans were expert in handling diverse national groups, permitting them the greatest freedom in managing their own affairs. Among successive emperors, Julius Caesar stands out as one who encouraged medicine most effectively. For example, he extended Roman citizenship to all of those practicing the healing arts. This continued under other emperors. Luke, one of the New Testament writers, was a Greek physician with Roman citizenship under Caesar Augustus.

In this Roman era GALEN, also a Greek physician, became a Roman citizen about 160 A.D. He was as dominating in thought and medical personality in his day as Hip-

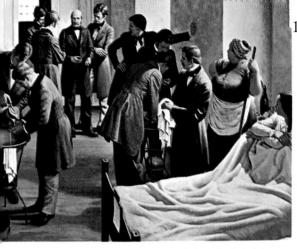

Philip Semmelweis (1818-1865), a Hungarian physician, found a way to prevent a fever that killed many mothers of new babies. The physicians simply had to wash their hands in a special solution, but many doctors objected to the procedure

pocrates had been before him. While a follower of Hippocratic thought, he departed from it by giving medicine a philosophic link. In this he was probably influenced by the philosopher Plato, whose teaching and writings were greatly respected. Another influence felt and spread by Galen was the use of certain botanical substances as curative agents. This was quite logical as examined today and one realizes the effect of Arabian thought after Alexandria fell and the Arabs took over the Greek areas, which passed into Moslem hands. Arabian physicians had developed skill in crude pharmacology.

The teachings of Galen were accepted as standard for nearly a thousand years. Universities came into being during this time. Those at Pisa and Padua in Italy and Montpellier in France became famous.

Although ANATOMY and PHYSIOLOGY became better known, not much progress in conquering disease was made until after the Middle Ages. Medicine, as always, had its devoted students and to them man owes a great deal for longevity and freedom from devastating disease. HARVEY, credited with discovery of the circulation of the blood in 1628, studied at Padua. Michael Servetus, who preceded Harvey in studies of the circulation, studied at Lyon, France. His work on the blood occurred almost 100 years before Harvey, but it was not recognized because Servetus was burned at the stake.

The work of LEEUWENHOEK, who perfected the MICROSCOPE of Jansen and Roger Bacon, made possible the discovery by MALPIGHI in 1661 of the circulation of the blood through arteries, capillaries, and veins. JENNER, by use of cowpox, almost eradicated SMALLPOX. PASTEUR, working with the phenomena of fermentation, led LISTER to think of cutting down germ infection in the operating room by use of antiseptics. KOCH, who discovered the tubercle bacillus, improved bacteriologic research.

With the discovery of germs as the cause of many diseases came ways of combating them with many different types of medicine. The general health of modern society has been greatly improved by an understanding of the principles of hygiene, both public and personal.

MODERN MEDICINE

Until recent years, the total medical needs of many people were the responsibility of a single physician. Today, however, health care professionals specialize in hundreds of different fields. The complexity of modern health care techniques and facilities simply makes it impossible for one physician or any trained worker to master more than a few areas.

Specialization allows sophisticated medical procedures to reach the greatest number of people in need of them. But the cost of such specialization, and the elaborate instruments and other facilities of modern health care centers, is staggering. In many developed nations, health care accounts for about ten percent of the gross national product. In recent years it has become increasingly difficult for many people, and even for large medical insurance companies, to pay for the high costs of health care. Many nations have developed national health insurance policies in an attempt to both provide full coverage for all citizens and to limit total health cost increases. During his 1992 campaign, U.S. President Bill Clinton made reducing health care costs his number one priority.

H.K.S./J.H.

SEE ALSO: ANTIBIOTICS, BACTERIOLOGY, BIOPHYSICS, CHEMOTHERAPY, DRUGS, PHARMACOLOGY, SURGERY

Medulla The medulla is the center of an organ like the ADRENAL gland or the center of the "stems" or stipes of brown ALGAE. The word also refers to the MEDULLA OBLONGATA of the brain, or to the bone marrow.

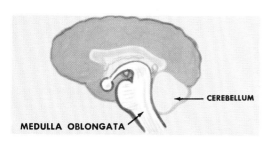

Location of the medulla oblongata

Medulla oblongata The medulla oblongata is the part of the BRAIN that connects with the spinal cord. The cavity of the cord continues into the medulla and widens out. In the medulla the cavity is known as the *fourth ventricle*.

In man there are twelve pairs of nerves connected to the brain. These nerves are called the *cranial nerves* and carry messages (impulses) from the sense organs to the brain. They also carry messages from the brain to the body cells which are going to respond. The medulla is important because many of the cranial nerves arise from it, and nerve centers that control reflexes connected with such functions as respiration and heart beat are located there.

Most brain tissue consists of tracts or groups of fibers which make connections with the nuclei of the brain. The nuclei consist of one or more cell bodies of nerve cells.

The medulla contains the nuclei of four of the cranial nerves. The *ninth* cranial nerve (glossopharyngeal) innervates (carries impulses to or from the brain) the tongue, pharynx, and tonsils. The *tenth* nerve (vagus) sends branches to the lungs, esophagus and heart. The *eleventh* (accessory) innervates the neck muscles, larynx, or voice box, and vocal cords. The *twelfth* (hypoglossal) goes to the tongue.

Reflexes concerned with vomiting, chewing, coughing, closing the eyelids, and sneezing arise from the nuclei of the cranial nerves.

Some of the groups of nerve cells which have an automatic control over some of the body functions have their centers in the medulla. There is a *cardiac center* to regulate the heart beat, a *respiratory center* to control the lungs, a *vasomotor center* to regulate the size in diameter of the blood vessels and others.

In addition to the nuclei, the main sensory and motor tracts betwen the SPINAL CORD and brain pass through the medulla. J. C. K.
SEE ALSO: AUTONOMIC NERVOUS SYSTEM, NERVOUS SYSTEM

Medusa see Coelenterata

Meiosis see Mitosis and meiosis

Meitner, Lise see Hahn, Otto

Melon Melon is the popular name for the fruit of several climbing or trailing plants. The most common melons are *muskmelon* and *watermelon.*

Muskmelon, often called *cantaloupe,* was native to Asia but now is being cultivated in all tropical, subtropical, and many temperate climates. It has long, running, prickly vines, and roundish, heart-shaped leaves, and small, yellow flowers. The fruit of the muskmelon has a hard, warty, or scaly rind and the flesh is juicy, sweet, and, most commonly, yellow or orange in color. In the center of the fruit, a pepo, are a great number of seeds from which the melons are propagated. In this group is the *honeydew* .

The watermelon VINE produces a large, sweet-tasting, seed-filled fruit. The vines are hairy and long-running and have light green leaves. Watermelons may weigh from 20 to 50 pounds (9.07 to 22.68 kilograms). Melons need a light, sandy soil, sunlight, and plant food. J.K.K.
SEE ALSO: FRUIT

Melt see Physical states and changes

Membrane see Meninges, Mucous membrane, Pericardium, Peritonitis

Muskmelon (left) and watermelon (right) are the most common melons

Gregor Mendel

Memory Memory is the ability to recall or bring back to mind past experiences. The loss of memory is called *amnesia.*
SEE ALSO: PSYCHOLOGY

Mendel, Gregor Johann (MEN-duhl, GRAY-gohr) (1822-1884) Gregor Mendel was a botanist, an Austrian monk of the Augustinian order who first formulated the laws of heredity, now called the *Mendelian Laws.* Experimenting with garden peas in his small monastery garden, he worked out certain laws which laid the foundation for the study of HEREDITY. However, Mendel's importance was not realized until 1900.

Born in Heinzendorf, Austria, Mendel developed an early interest in science. After having studied for two years at the Philosophical Institute at Olmutz, he entered an Augustinian monastery at Brunn. During his training to become a monk, he taught himself science. Then after having taught Greek and mathematics for a short time, he was sent by his abbot to the University of Vienna where he studied physics, chemistry, mathematics, zoology, and botany. Returning to Brunn, he taught natural science in the technical high school until he was elected abbot of his monastery by his fellow monks. It was during this period that he carried on his experimentation with garden peas.

After Mendel became an abbot, his experimental research almost stopped because of his pressing administrative duties. However, he had already written his paper discussing the ideas of unit-characteristics, and dominant versus recessive action of inherited traits. It had been published two years earlier by the local Society of Natural Science. Yet fame did not come to Gregor Mendel until 1900, sixteen years after his death, when three other European botanists independently obtained results similar to Mendel's. It was while searching through experimental data previously published that they found Mendel's paper, and for the first time the world realized the importance of this obscure abbot. Revered and loved by his fellow monks and the townsfolk, Mendel was a scientist whose greatness no one had ever suspected. D. H. J.
SEE ALSO: EVOLUTION, ZOOLOGY

Mendeleev's Periodic Table (men-duh-LAY-uhf) In 1869, Dmitri Mendeleev proposed a law of chemistry called the *periodic law.* He said that when the ELEMENTS are arranged in order of increasing atomic weight, they periodically repeat certain characteristics. He illustrated this by arranging the elements in seven groups, or periods. Those elements listed below these seven elements had similar properties to the one above. The periodic table is a foundation stone of modern CHEMISTRY.

Mendeleev's conclusion is amazing when the lack of information at that time is considered. Only at the beginning of the nineteenth century was the difference between an element and a COMPOUND discovered. In the following decade, there was a great growth of facts about individual elements and compounds. These facts needed to be organized and related.

In 1817, J. W. Dobereiner showed that there was a weight relationship between three groups of three elements. He called the three elements of a group a *triad.* Between 1828 and 1854, more elements were discovered, and some of the triads then had four members.

In 1863, J. A. R. Newlands divided the elements into seven groups related to the first seven known elements. He called these groups *octaves,* after the musical octave which repeats every seven notes.

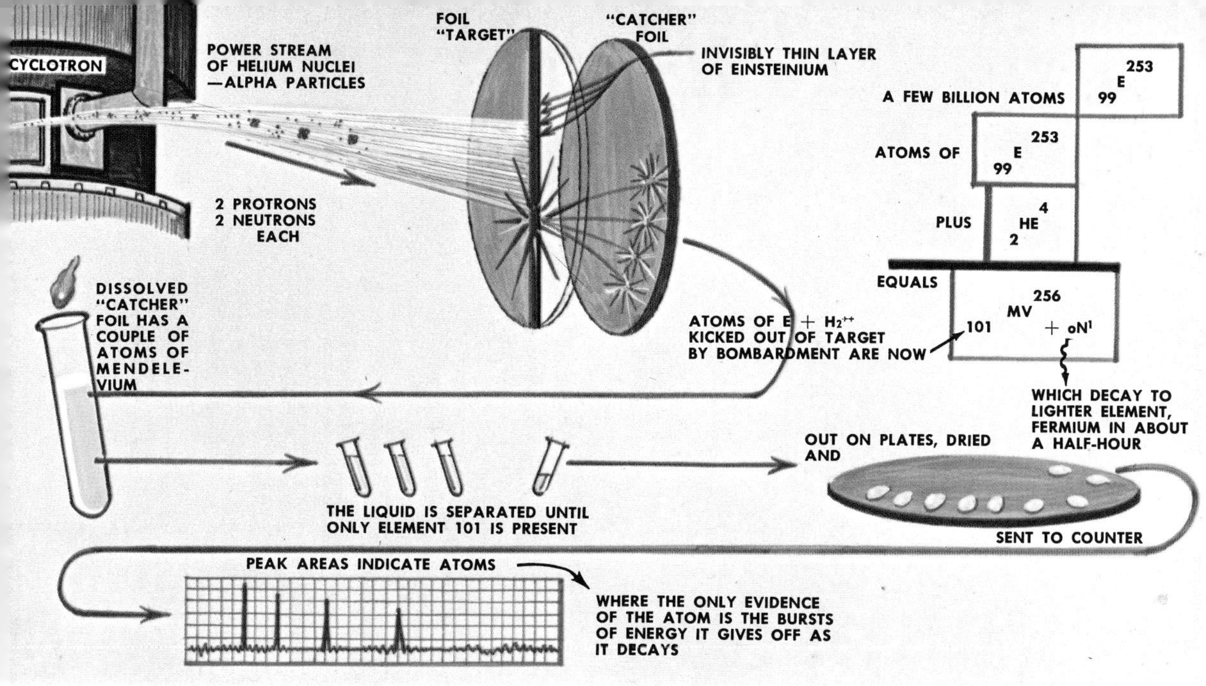
CYCLOTRON
POWER STREAM OF HELIUM NUCLEI —ALPHA PARTICLES
FOIL "TARGET"
"CATCHER" FOIL
INVISIBLY THIN LAYER OF EINSTEINIUM
A FEW BILLION ATOMS
253 E 99
ATOMS OF
253 E 99
PLUS
4 HE 2
EQUALS
256 MV 101 + oN1
2 PROTRONS 2 NEUTRONS EACH
DISSOLVED "CATCHER" FOIL HAS A COUPLE OF ATOMS OF MENDELEVIUM
ATOMS OF E + H2++ KICKED OUT OF TARGET BY BOMBARDMENT ARE NOW
WHICH DECAY TO LIGHTER ELEMENT, FERMIUM IN ABOUT A HALF-HOUR
OUT ON PLATES, DRIED AND
THE LIQUID IS SEPARATED UNTIL ONLY ELEMENT 101 IS PRESENT
SENT TO COUNTER
PEAK AREAS INDICATE ATOMS
WHERE THE ONLY EVIDENCE OF THE ATOM IS THE BURSTS OF ENERGY IT GIVES OFF AS IT DECAYS

Since elements such as mendelevium are not free in nature, scientists must devise ways to prove they exist and to produce them

Before Mendeleev, all this work was done in an attempt to classify elements. Mendeleev proposed a law of nature in his work. He discovered a fundamental characteristic that was always true of all elements. On the basis of this law, Mendeleev correctly predicted six new elements and revealed errors in the atomic weights of other known elements. The unifying properties on which he based his analysis included atomic weight, VALENCE, and chemical properties. He correctly noted the difference between members of the same group, as for example, potassium and copper. In a later chart he proposed eight groups. The main change in the periodic table today is that the atomic number, rather than the atomic weight, serves to establish the sequence of the elements. J. K. L.

SEE ALSO: ATOM; COMPOUNDS, STABILITY OF

Mendelevium (men-duh-LEE-vee-um) Mendelevium is an element whose chemical symbol is Md. It belongs to the ACTINIDE series of elements and does not occur in nature. Its atomic number is 101.

In 1952 University of California scientists discovered and prepared mendelevium by artificial nuclear TRANSMUTATION of a lighter element. An einsteinium isotope was bombarded with helium nuclei accelerated in a cyclotron. The nuclei combined, forming the mendelevium isotope Md^{256}. It is expected that all mendelevium isotopes will be radioactive, and their maximum half-lives will probably be in days. Its most stable isotope has a mass number of 256. Less than one-millionth of a gram has been available for experimentation. D. L. D.

SEE ALSO: ATOM, ELEMENTS

Mendelian Laws see Heredity; Mendel, Gregor Johann

Meninges (muh-NINN-gees) Meninges are the membranes covering the BRAIN and SPINAL CORD. The three membranes covering the parts of the brain are the *dura mater, arachnoid,* and *pia mater*. The meninges furnish protection, blood, and drainage.

SEE: NERVOUS SYSTEM

Meningitis (menn-in-JYE-tiss) Meningitis is an inflammation of the membranes (meninges) covering the brain and spinal cord.

It can be caused by BACTERIA, VIRUSES, FUNGI, YEASTS, PARASITES, or the body's own cells (for example, leukemic meningitis). The infection is often carried by the bloodstream, but it can enter directly through an open wound. EPIDEMIC meningitis is caused by a bacterium. A vaccine is being developed to combat it. E.S.S.

Menstruation (menn-stroo-AY-shunn) Menstruation is the term applied to the periodic discharge of blood from the womb or uterus of the human female. This normal function of the body usually starts between the ages of 11 and 16 years and continues at regular intervals until the age of about 45 years. The word "menstruation" comes from the Latin word meaning "month." The usual interval between periods is 28 days although variation from 20 to 35 days must be considered within the normal limits. The flow lasts from three to five days.

The first appearance of the discharge is one of the signs of approaching maturity. Other signs are a change in body contour and particularly in the breast structure. Accompanying behavior and emotional changes awaken in the newly-developing young woman.

The monthly reappearance of the flow may be accompanied in a few individuals by discomfort. There may be a feeling of fullness in the breasts or abdomen or an irregularity of the bowel function.

Menstruation occurs after the development and discharge of the EGG or ovum. The inner cellular lining of the uterus is rejuvenated with a fresh supply of blood as part of the preparation for the reception in the Fallopian tubes of an egg properly fertilized by a male SPERM. When such fertilization does not take place, the uterus discharges these engorged cells and is ready for a new cycle. Menstruation, then, depends upon the regular development of the egg—a process called OVULATION—or its discharge.

Periodic menstruation normally continues throughout the years of life during which conception is possible. It is intimately linked to the operation of glands which supply the internal secretions. The ovaries are both stimulated and inhibited in their activity by the PITUITARY gland which lies at the base of the brain. H. K. S.
SEE ALSO: ESTROUS CYCLE, FERTILIZATION, REPRODUCTIVE SYSTEMS

Mercury (element) Mercury is a heavy, silver-colored ELEMENT. It is the only common metal which is LIQUID at room temperatures. Mercury vapor and many mercury compounds are poisonous.

Mercury occurs in nature but is principally obtained from an ore called CINNABAR, a red sulfide of mercury. This is heated, and vapors of the element are condensed and processed to purity.

Mercury is useful for THERMOMETERS, as it does not cling to the walls of the tube. Since it has a higher BOILING POINT than alcohol, it is used where temperatures are high. Mercury is also used in BAROMETERS, where its weight is desirable, because the atmosphere supports a column 30 inches (76.2 centimeters) high.

Mercury can combine with other metals by being worked into them. These combinations are called *amalgams.* Dentists use amalgams of silver and gold for fillings.

Mercury (symbol Hg from Latin *hydrargyrum)* has atomic number 80. Its atomic weight is 200.59. Its oxide is an orange-red powder.

The poisonous nature of mercury has been known for generations. Victims of mercury poisoning exhibit physical, mental, and emotional disorders.

Mercury comes into the environment from many sources. Industry and agriculture are two major sources. Industrial processes, such as the decomposition of sodium chloride or the production of plastics, release large amounts of mercury. Organic mercury compounds have been used extensively as seed coatings to prevent the formation of molds and fungi.

Once in the environment, the mercury is converted into organic compounds by anaerobic bacteria. The organo-metallic compounds then move through the food chain to higher animals. D.J.I./A.J.H.
SEE ALSO: ATOM, ELEMENTS

Mercury (planet) Mercury is the closest planet to the sun. Its diameter is 3,008 miles (4840.9 kilometers), only slightly more than the Earth's moon. Its surface features seem to resemble those of the Moon.

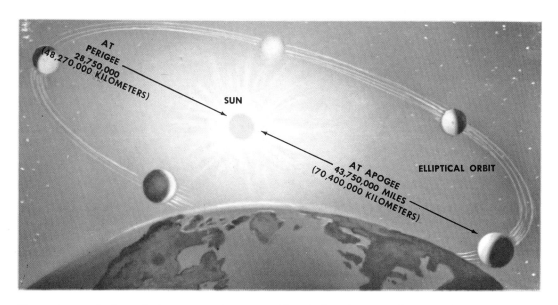

Mercury's speed of revolution causes the same side of the planet to be turned toward the sun throughout the orbit. Thus, a year is also a day on Mercury, both equal to 88 Earth days

Mercury revolves around the sun once in 88 days. Its period of rotation is 58.6 days. This would mean that one side of the planet is facing the sun most of the time. Because of this, the surface facing the sun reaches a temperature of about 700° F. (371.1° C.), hot enough to melt lead. The side away from the sun is intensely cold, probably as low as −450° F. (−267.8° C.), which is very close to ABSOLUTE ZERO. Since Mercury is so small its gravitational pull must be very low.

Mercury has essentially no ATMOSPHERE. Its mass is so small that its gravity pull is too low to hold on to any gases for atmosphere. Sound waves need atmosphere to travel; so visitors to Mercury would have to communicate by radio.

At different times of the year, Mercury can be seen in the eastern sky before sunrise and in the western sky shortly after sunset. As viewed from the Earth, Mercury exhibits *phases* similar to the moon. Since Mercury has extremes of temperature between its light side and the side away from the sun, it is doubtful that any type of life, as we know it, could survive. If man ever travels to Mercury, he will probably land in the *twilight zone,* the area lying between the extremes of temperature.

Mercury's orbit is not circular. It is ellipti-

cal. Mercury's path looks like the outline of an egg. Because of the elliptical orbit, Mercury's distance from the sun varies. At its closest point to the sun, Mercury is 28,750,-000 miles (46,268,640 kilometers) from the sun. Its greatest distance from the sun is 43,750,000 miles (70,408,800 kilometers).

Mercury's speed varies according to its distance from the sun. When it is near the sun, it travels almost 36 miles (57.9 kilometers) per second. When it is farthest from the sun it slows down to less than 25 miles (40.2 kilometers) per second—still very fast.

Mercury can be seen with the naked eye. At the proper time it can be seen about two hours after sunset or about two hours before sunrise. It cannot be seen at night because it is near the sun, and at night the Earth faces away from the sun. Sometimes astronomers study Mercury during the day, but their telescopes have to be pointed in the right direction, and some of the light from the sun has to be filtered off. Special precautions are taken to protect their eyes because it is very dangerous to look directly at the sun with a telescope.

Mercury's orbit is not on the same plane as the Earth's. It is inclined (tilted) a little. Sometimes Mercury seems to travel above the sun, sometimes below, and sometimes it goes across the sun. When Mercury passes across the sun—between the Earth and the sun—it makes a small black dot on the sun. If it were a large planet, it would cause an ECLIPSE. At these times Mercury is said to be "in transit." Mercury will transit the sun on November 14, 1999.

Because of the position, shape, and incline of Mercury's orbit and its orbital speed, Mercury's position in the sky changes rapidly. When it is east of the sun, it is visible as a *morning star;* when it is west of the sun, it is an *evening star.*

Mercury is so far away, and close to the sun that it is not a very good target for even the largest telescopes. Prior to the 1973 Mariner 10 mission to Mercury, little was known about its surface features. The camera on board the spacecraft took over 2,000 images of a heavily cratered and generally rugged *terrain* similar to the Earth's moon. The CALORIS BASIN on Mercury resembles many of the large impact basins on the Moon. It too was produced by a collision with a large asteroid-sized object, but unlike the Moon it did not fill in with *lava.* Another unusual feature of Mercury is its DENSITY. For a planet ⅓ the size of the Earth, it has an equal density. This fact indicates that most of Mercury's interior must be composed of a heavy metallic core, with only a thin rocky crust covering it. It is generally believed that Mercury's surface is composed of BASALT, the same material that covers much of the Earth and Moon.

C.L.K./P.P.S.

SEE ALSO: ASTRONOMY, MOON, SOLAR SYSTEM

Mercury barometer see Barometer

Merganser see Ducks

Meridian A meridian is an imaginary line running north and south from pole to pole on the earth's surface. LONGITUDE is measured east and west from the prime meridian at Greenwich, England, to the 180th meridian (the International Date Line).

SEE ALSO: EARTH; GEOGRAPHY; POLES, NORTH AND SOUTH; TIME ZONES

Meristem Meristem is a group of cells that can divide to produce growth in a PLANT. The *apical* meristem at ROOT and STEM tips causes growth in length and the *lateral* meristem (CAMBIUM) enlarges stem diameter.

SEE: PLANT TISSUES

James P. Rowan

A mesa has a flat top and very steep sides. A butte is a small mesa

Mesa (MAY-suh) In the Americas, a mesa is found in dry DESERT lands. Mesas are formed on a high upland PLATEAU of small to moderate size. They have a flat top and steep sides.

Mesas usually are portions of larger plateaus that have been detached by the formation and widening of canyons or arroyos. An *arroyo* is the Spanish name applied to flat-bottomed, steep-sided valleys.

A resistant layer of rock, such as sandstone or some form of solidified lava, usually forms the top part of a mesa. The more rapid EROSION of a less resistant rock beneath is responsible for the table-like appearance of this plateau feature. The resistant layer remains and forms the mesa. Formations of similar origin but smaller in size are called *buttes.*

Mesas are quite characteristic of New Mexico and Arizona. Buttes are found usually in Montana, the Dakotas, and Wyoming.

V. V. N.

SEE ALSO: CANYON, GEOLOGY

Mesoderm see Cleavage, Embryology

Meson (MAY-sohn) A meson is a NUCLEAR PARTICLE which has a mass between that of an electron and proton and carries a positive, negative or neutral charge. Several different kinds have been found with different weights and characteristics.

SEE: NUCLEAR SCIENCE

Mesophyll see Leaves

Mesothorium see Thorium

Mesozoic Era (mess-uh-ZOH-ick) Mesozoic Era is the age of the dinosaurs, the "middle" time era in the earth's history. It lasted about 160 million years, between the PALEOZOIC ERA of ancient life and the CENOZOIC ERA of modern plant and animal life.

A long period of erosion was followed by great floods. Mountain building began along the Pacific Coast from Alaska to South America. Pines and flowering plants were new developments. Reptiles were the most important form of animal life in numbers and in kinds. Insects and the first gliding birds appeared. Mesozoic rock layers formed the source of the Gulf Coast, Arabian, and Venezuelan oil.

Triassic Period was the earliest of the time periods, known for the "red beds" or the red sediment deposited on the land areas through erosion. Volcanoes occurred throughout the Southern Hemisphere, and in Brazil there was an immense area of lava rock. The Hudson River Palisades are a Triassic formation, and the PETRIFIED FOREST in Arizona shows the cone-bearing trees of this period.

The cold seas at first limited marine life, but later mollusks, clams, oysters, starfish, and sea urchins were present. The first turtles and the first reptiles that adapted to life on land are the important new animal forms. In August of 1960 three high school boys digging in a Triassic rock quarry near New York City found an unusual fossil thought to be the very first gliding reptile, older by 30 million years than other finds.

During the *Jurassic Period,* continued erosion and the formation of fresh water lakes and coal beds occurred. The seas contained the first true crabs, barnacles, and increasing animal life. DINOSAURS dominated the land and grew to huge sizes. This is sometimes called the *age of the cycads,* for these palm-like plants occurred abundantly. The GINGKO may be the oldest of the seed plants living today. There were also true pines and sequoias.

During the 65 million year *Cretaceous Period* great flooding cut North America

The tyrannosaurus was a giant reptile of the Mesozoic Era

into two islands, east and west; the Gulf of Mexico nearly reached the Ohio River. Volcanoes and FOLDING began the uplift that continued for millions of years to form the *cordilleran* mountain chain through both Americas.

Marine animals increasingly became mobile and equipped with claws and teeth for more efficient food-getting. Flowering plants (ANGIOSPERMS) were the new forms of plant life. With them came the development of insects. A wasp nest fossil dating back to this time has been found. This period marks the end of the dinosaurs and the increase in mammals.   A.P.M.

SEE ALSO: EVOLUTION, GEOLOGIC TIME TABLE, GYMNOSPERM

Mesquite (muhs-KEYT) Mesquite are tropical or subtropical thorny trees or shrubs. They belong to the PEA family. There are about twenty-five species. They have small greenish flowers and leathery, very narrow non-splitting pods. The most common mesquite is a thorny shrub that grows only a few feet (or centimeters) high.

SEE ALSO: LEGUME

Mesquite

Metabolimeter (met-tuh-BAHL-uh-meeter) A doctor needs to know whether a person's body is burning too little fuel for necessary energy. He can find this out by knowing the person's basal METABOLISM, or the least amount of energy it takes to keep the body at normal body temperature. The metabolimeter determines basal metabolism by measuring the amount of oxygen the person's body uses while lying still.

Metabolism (muh-TAB-uh-lizm) Metabolism is the process by which living things grow and repair their bodies and produce energy needed for life. Metabolism includes all the chemical changes that take place in the protoplasm of the CELL. The changes which build up new protoplasm from simpler materials are called *anabolic* metabolism. The changes which break down parts of the protoplasm are *catabolic* metabolism.

All metabolic processes use food as the raw material for supplying ENERGY and building new tissues. Foods include water, minerals, VITAMINS, CARBOHYDRATES (starches and sugars), PROTEINS, and FATS. The latter three are changed by digestion to simple sugar, AMINO ACIDS, FATTY ACIDS, and glycogen, which can be assimilated. Glucose, fats and amino acids may be used to form a basic part of protoplasm, oxidized to give the body the heat and energy it needs, or stored for future use.

In plants there are four anabolic processes and two catabolic processes. PLANT cells produce sugars and starches from carbon dioxide and water in PHOTOSYNTHESIS. They recombine the atoms of some of these carbohydrates to produce fats and proteins. Plant cells can change any of these food substances into compounds which can be stored. Plants are able to grow and repair worn out or injured parts by converting amino acids, carbohydrates, and fat in living protoplasm. This conversion is called *synthesis*.

The catabolic processes of plants are

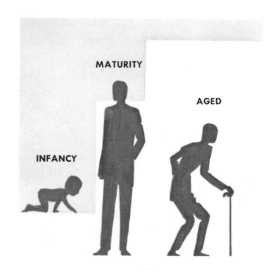

CATABOLISM (DE-STRUCTIVE METABOLISM)   ANABOLISM (CON-STRUCTIVE METABOLISM)

respiration and *digestion*. Respiration is the chemical combination of foods with oxygen releasing the stored energy of foods. This energy is necessary for further chemical changes and movement. Digestion in the cell changes complex foods into simpler food which can be oxidized in respiration, used for growth, or changed and stored.

Animal digestion is a catabolic process. Food is taken in and broken down into simpler chemicals by the process of digestion. In protozoans, sponges, and partly in coelenterates, digestion is a process occurring within the cells. In higher animals food is digested outside the cell and the cell absorbs the predigested food. Forty per cent of digested carbohydrates and fats, and eighty to eighty-five per cent of digested proteins are oxidized in the cell to produce energy. The rest are stored as body fat or glycogen. Proteins not used in repair are changed to carbohydrates and oxidized or stored. Amino acids from protein are recombined into proteins characteristic of the animal. When an organism is performing its normal functions, metabolism is carried on at a uniform rate. When one has not eaten for several hours and lies quietly, metabolism is carried on at a slow rate, called the *basal metabolic rate*. This rate in humans is twenty to twenty-five per cent greater in children than adults, and eight per cent higher in males. It declines slowly after age twenty. Basal metabolic rate is largely controlled by the THYROID gland.   J. K. L.

SEE ALSO: DIGESTIVE SYSTEM

Metacarpal bone see Skeleton

Metal Metals are useful to man because they can be formed and shaped more easily than stone. Many of them have greater strength for their weight than other materials, and they lend themselves to a very wide variety of uses.

In fact, it may very well be said that our present civilization would not be possible without metals.

Actually, historians do not consider the human race to have become civilized until it had learned the use of metals. The term "Stone Age" people simply refers to those who did not know how to use metals.

Even today there are some peoples who are so primitive that uses of metals are unknown to them, and they must be classed as stone age peoples.

It appears that use of metals began as early as 5,000 years ago when the Egyptians used copper for utensils.

The earliest people who used metals could take advantage only of those metals, such as copper and gold, which are found in almost pure form in chunks or nuggets, perhaps just scattered around in places where the metals occurred.

One of the great discoveries of mankind was that these chunks of metal could be changed into more useful or more ornamental shapes by beating or pounding. Although the tools and equipment have changed greatly, the basic principle of shaping metal in this way has not changed in 5,000 years.

When early explorers came to South America, they were surprised that the Indians were using gold for very common purposes. The Indians valued it because it was useful and not because it was scarce.

Much later, the first explorers in the upper peninsula of Michigan found the Indians hammering copper from the great Michigan copper deposits in much the same way as the ancient Chaldeans and Egyp-

J. Daniel Willems

Cassiterite, the principal ore of tin, an important metal, is a dioxide of tin, SnO_2

tians had done thousands of years before. The earliest copper workings are dated about 3,500 years before Christ.

EXTRACTING THE METALS

In many areas where people began to use metals early, the supply appeared to be used up. Then it was discovered that smaller quantities of metals were to be found in rocks or even in the earth. That is, the metals they wanted were mixed in with other minerals, and it seemed impossible to separate the wanted from the unwanted.

This problem of how to remove the rock and earth or other minerals and obtain the particular metal sought is that of *extraction.* Copper was the first metal to be extracted from its surrounding minerals.

From that time on the story of metals has been the finding of new metals, the discovery of new methods of extracting them and finding new uses for metals.

One recently discovered metal, URANIUM, has given us the "atomic age." It is of great importance in weapons production and as a nuclear fuel. Uranium is in the earth's crust and extraction begins by pulverizing the ore. The ore then undergoes extensive chemical concentration. The process returns about 6.6 lbs. (30 kg) of uranium per 2.2 tons (1,000 kg) of ore.

Some metals are becoming scarce, especially the *high-grade ores.* These are ores in which the proportion of the desired metal to other minerals is very high. This means that much usable metal can be obtained from a relatively small amount of ore. It is so expensive to obtain metal from *low-grade ore* that mining operations usually stop after the better grade deposits have been worked out.

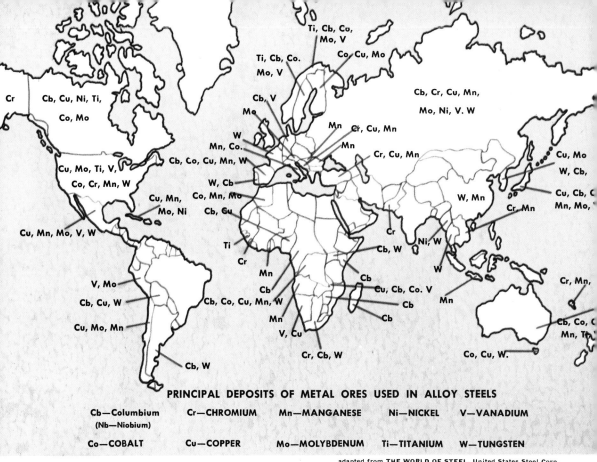

PRINCIPAL DEPOSITS OF METAL ORES USED IN ALLOY STEELS

Cb—Columbium	Cr—CHROMIUM	Mn—MANGANESE	Ni—NICKEL	V—VANADIUM
(Nb—Niobium)				
Co—COBALT	Cu—COPPER	Mo—MOLYBDENUM	Ti—TITANIUM	W—TUNGSTEN

adapted from **THE WORLD OF STEEL**, United States Steel Corp.

When better ores are completely exhausted or hard to get, the use of low-grade ores may be necessary or more practical. Sometimes new methods of extracting these can be found, as a way to lower the costs. This is true of the new processes for the handling of low-grade iron ore called *taconite,* found in quantities in Michigan, Wisconsin and Minnesota.

Many metals need to be *concentrated* in order to make them ready for extraction.

With some ores *crushing* and *grinding* will be sufficient to concentrate the metal. Another method used is *gravitational separation.* This takes advantage of the fact that some ores are heavier than their surrounding minerals and will settle first in water. The unwanted minerals then settle on top and can be removed easily.

Froth flotation is still another concentration process. This involves mixing oil and water with the ground ore and blowing air through until an oily froth forms, to which the particles of ore will cling.

Electrostatic concentration and *magnetic concentration* take advantage of the fact that certain finely crushed ores can be pulled from other unwanted minerals by attraction of electrostatic or magnetic currents.

Other ores are concentrated by *chemical* means, such as precipitation.

After ores have been concentrated, the processes of extracting the metals involve great heat, electrical current, chemical or other means. A well-known example is the *blast furnace* for steel, although electrical methods are now becoming prominent in the steel industry. Another prominent extracting technique is the *electrolytic* method which made the modern aluminum industry possible.

The number and uses of metals have increased tremendously since the time of the first primitive man who picked up a shiny gold nugget and admired it as an ornament for his person.

WORKING METALS

Very early peoples found, probably by accident, that metals could be melted by heat and poured hot into various forms or molds. Some of the metal statues which were formed that way in early time and which have been preserved for us to examine show a very high degree of skill in such work.

Casting and molding are still important methods of working metals.

Early metal workers also found that in many cases *impure* metals, such as copper

1050

mixed with another metal to make bronze, were superior to the pure metals, in such ways as strength and hardness. These combinations of metals are called *alloys*.

Today metals are sprayed, squirted, stretched, pounded, powdered and treated with a wide variety of techniques.

The "squirting" technique of metals is called *extrusion*. It is very similar to squeezing toothpaste out of a tube. The form of the metal coming out depends on the size and shape of the opening through which it is being forced. When hardened, these metal shapes can be cut off in the desired lengths or finished in other ways.

The metals used in wire making are an essential part of modern life, with wire being used for such widely different purposes as carrying telephone messages and forming nails. Wire generally is formed by pulling rods of the desired metal through openings which are made gradually smaller until the desired thickness of wire is created. Wires which are almost invisible are formed by pulling the metal through holes in diamonds.

Sintering and *deep drawing* are other metal processes. Metal workers are also concerned with methods of fastening metals together, such as welding, brazing, soldering and, lately, even gluing.

Protection of metals from CORROSION is done in many ways, from simple painting to complicated chemical treatment.

Metals in commonest use today are IRON, ALUMINUM, and COPPER. Other most-used metals include ZINC, MAGNESIUM, TIN, LEAD, and NICKEL. About 27 other metals are generally considered to have commercial importance.

Commercially important metals include some which are not mined in great quantities but which have critical uses nevertheless. A good example of these is TUNGSTEN. Two of its principal uses are for the lighting filament in electric lamps, and in combination with *carbides,* to form the finest metal-cutting tools.

Metals can be distinguished from other minerals by chemical means. In a solution, scientists have found that metals are *positive* in their electrical charge.   J. A. C.

SEE ALSO: ALLOY, CHEMISTRY, ELECTROLYSIS, ELEMENTS, MINERALOGY

Metalloid see Metal

✳ THINGS TO DO

WHICH METALS WILL REPLACE OTHERS FROM THEIR SALTS?

1 Dissolve a few copper sulfate crystals in a half tumbler of water. Place a steel table knife in this solution. What happens to the surface of the knife? The iron on it will go into solution. Then the copper accumulates on the surface of the utensil.

2 Place some iron screws in a salt solution of copper sulfate. The copper in the solution soon will collect on the iron.

3 Place a piece of fresh aluminum foil in soapy water overnight. Next day note its dull color. Sandpaper will clean off the oxide coating again. Aluminum plus oxygen produces aluminum oxide.

4 Some metals react with water and replace some of the hydrogen. Hydroxides are formed as hydrogen is given off.

Metallurgy Metallurgy is the science of extracting metals from their ores, refining them, and adapting them for use. This includes many techniques, such as alloying, heat treating, plating, or other procedures to make metals suitable for their intended purpose.
SEE ALSO: METAL

Metamorphic rock see Rocks

Metamorphosis of a frog: tadpole to adult.

Metamorphosis Metamorphosis is the change in body form and structure which takes place in some animals as they develop from young (larvae) to adult. The word "metamorphosis" comes from a Greek word which means "to transform." Grasshoppers, termites, dragonflies, damselflies, and frogs go through an *incomplete metamorphosis* in which there is a partial change of body form. Bees, beetles, flies, fleas, moths, butterflies, and doodlebugs go through a *complete metamorphosis* in which there are three stages of change in body form and structure. These three stages are: *larva, pupa,* and *adult.*

Baby grasshoppers are called *nymphs,* and undergo incomplete metamorphosis. With their six legs and compound eyes, they look somewhat like adult grasshoppers, except for their wings. The nymph's wings grow very slowly, getting a little bigger each time the nymph molts (sheds its outer covering). The wings are not fully developed until the GRASSHOPPER has reached the adult stage.

The life cycle of the FROG is generally used as an example of incomplete metamorphosis among animals. In the spring the female frog lays eggs in a pond or stream. Frogs in the form of *tadpoles* hatch from these eggs. Tadpoles have long tails and no legs. They breathe by means of GILLS and must live in water. After a period of time, the tadpoles gradually begin to lose their gills and tails, to develop legs and LUNGS, and to take on the form of adult frogs. Changes also take place inside the bodies of the tadpoles. They do not eat during this period of change.

The life cycle of a butterfly is an example of *complete metamorphosis.* The adult female butterfly lays eggs on the leaf of a plant. From these eggs emerge butterflies in the form of crawling *larvae* called caterpillars. The caterpillars have many legs, biting jaws, and no wings. They may be brown, yellow, white, or green with black rings. They eat and grow for about two months, shedding their skin (molting) many times as their body increases in size. The butterflies, still in the form of CATERPILLARS, then form a smooth hard case (*chrysalis*) about themselves and hang from a twig or leaf. The larvae of some insects, such as the moth, spin a thick web called a COCOON about their bodies, fastening themselves to a twig or rough spot. This is the *pupa stage.* Later, they emerge as adults.   D.J.A.

SEE ALSO: BEE, BEETLES, BUTTERFLY, DRAGONFLY, FLY, LARVA, MOLTING, MOTHS

Metaphase see Mitosis and Meiosis

Metatarsal see Skeleton

Metazoan see Zoology

Metchnikoff, Elie (1845-1916) Elie Metchnikoff, a Russian biologist and PAUL EHRLICH won the 1908 NOBEL PRIZE in physiology and medicine.

Metchnikoff devoted his life to science. He was most renowned as a bacteriologist. His early career was spent in teaching zoology. He then took up private research. He studied lower forms of life, the *invertebrates.* From his studies on sponges he proceeded to do work at the cellular level. He became interested in blood cells and microbes. Metchnikoff observed that certain cells were capable of ingesting solid particles. His studies of *phagocytosis* and *immunology* led to his being awarded the 1908 Nobel Prize.   A.J.H.

Meteor Meteors are often called "falling stars" or "shooting stars," but they are not stars at all. Meteors are small pieces of rock or metal that have been pulled into Earth's atmosphere by gravity. As they pass through the atmosphere they glow very brightly as they burn up. Occasionally, a meteor fragment may reach the Earth's surface intact. It then becomes a *meteorite*.

Meteorites are broadly classified into three basic groups: the irons, stony-irons, and stones, based on the amounts of metal to rock material present in their composition. Iron meteorites are mainly composed of nickel-iron alloy minerals. They are extremely heavy for their size when compared to most Earth rocks, and they are strongly attracted to a MAGNET. Stony-irons are composed of half nickel-iron metal and half rock minerals. A special type of stony-iron called a *pallasite* is composed of large OLIVINE crystals embedded in the metal. These are relatively rare. Stone meteorites are the most common and are very similar to a volcanic rock called BASALT in their mineral compositions. Small spherules called *chondrules* are common to most stony meteorites, and this feature does not occur in any type of Earth rock. A unique type of stony meteorite called *carbonaceous chondrite* has been found to have several organic compounds in its chemistry. Some scientists believe that this type of meteorite may have been responsible for the beginning of life on Earth.

Meteorites are believed to have originated in the ASTEROID belt as fragments of a planet that never completely formed. Every year the Earth passes through meteoroid swarms that are the remains of old COMETS, and the result is the occurrence of a *meteor shower*.   P.P.S.

SEE ALSO: ASTEROIDS, CRATER, MOON

Meteors that fall to earth are called meteorites.

Wide World Photos

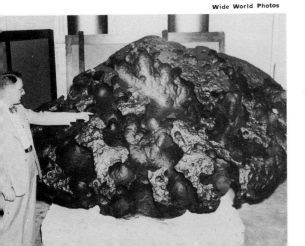

Methane molecule, CH_4

Methane (METH-ane) Methane is a colorless and odorless gas. It is found in large amounts in wells and mines in Texas, Oklahoma, Kansas, Kentucky, West Virginia, Pennsylvania, and parts of Canada (Alberta and Saskatchewan). It usually occurs with oil deposits. It is used as a major part of cooking and heating gas. Methane is also called "marsh gas."

Methane is an organic compound containing carbon and hydrogen. Its chemical formula is CH_4. It is the simplest and the first in a series of compounds called *hydrocarbons*. This series is continued by the addition of one carbon and two hydrogen atoms (CH_2). A new compound is formed with each such addition. *Propane* (C_3H_8) is one of the methane series.

The gas used in homes for cooking and heating is about eighty-five per cent methane. Methane is normally non-poisonous, but in the absence of oxygen a person inhaling methane can become asphyxiated. It can also form explosive mixtures with air if the mixture is made up of about one volume of methane to ten volumes of air.

Methane can be prepared in the laboratory. However, most methane is obtained commerically from NATURAL GAS. It is slightly soluble in water and very soluble in alcohol, ether, and other organic solvents. Its molecular weight is 16.04.   M.S.

SEE ALSO: HYDROCARBON, ORGANIC COMPOUNDS

Methane series Methane series, also called *paraffin* series, is a group of straight-chain hydrocarbons with the formula C_nH_{2n+2}. Methane (CH_4) is simplest. Some others are ethane (C_2H_6) and propane (C_3H_8). Their heat reactions make them good fuels.

SEE: HYDROCARBON

Methanol see Alcohol

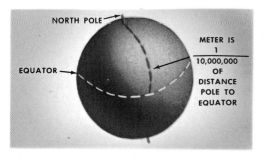

NORTH POLE

EQUATOR

METER IS 1 10,000,000 OF DISTANCE POLE TO EQUATOR

Metric system (METT-rick) In the late eighteenth century in France, a new system of measurement called the *metric system* was developed. This standard of length was related to the dimensions of the earth.

The units in the metric system were defined so that they were related to each other in units of ten:

mega means 1,000,000
myria means 10,000
kilo means 1,000
hecto means 100
deka means 10
deci means 1/10
centi means 1/100
milli means 1/1,000
micro means 1/1,000,000
millimicro means 1/1,000,000,000

The basic unit of length is the *meter;* thus, a kilometer is 1,000 meters and a centimeter is 1/100 of a meter. The basic unit for mass is a *gram* and the basic unit for capacity is a *liter*. Area is based on the square of a length measure, such as square meter and volume is based on the cube of a length measure, such as cubic centimeter. Temperature is measured on the Celsius (CENTIGRADE) scale with 0° as the freezing point of water and 100° as the boiling point.

In the metric system there is a relationship between the units of capacity, volume, and mass. One milliliter of a liquid is the same as one cubic centimeter of that liquid. In turn, one milliliter or one cubic centimeter of pure water weighs one gram (at a temperature of 4° C). M.M.L.

SEE ALSO: MEASUREMENT

Mica (MY-kuh) Mica is one of a group of MINERALS containing a form of the element SILICON. It is mined in large pieces called *books* which are separated into very thin transparent *leaves*.

Mica occurs in two basic forms: *muscovite,* which is clear and generally colorless, and *biotite,* which is black to brownish. Mica exhibits a combination of perfect cleavage, elasticity, and low thermal *conductivity*. Ninety percent of the production of sheet muscovite is used by the electrical industry for condensers, insulating material, and heating elements. P.P.S.

MICA

The mineral mica can be found in the ground in sheet form

Microbe A microbe is a unicellular plant or animal so small it cannot be seen without a microscope. The term includes PROTOZOA, ALGAE, fungi, BACTERIA, rickettsiae, and the viruses. Most grow and feed on other organisms (are *parasitic*), and some cause disease.

SEE ALSO: FUNGUS, PARASITE, VIRUS

Microfilm Microfilm is photographic FILM used to record printed matter on a very reduced scale. The image can later be enlarged and read on a special reader. Microfilm is useful because it reduces storage problems in libraries and offices.

SEE: PHOTOGRAPHY

Microgram see Measurement

Micrometer see Caliper

Microorganism (my-kroh-AWR-gun-izzuhm) *Micro* means small or one-millionth. *Organism* refers to any living thing. So, a *microorganism* is any organism that is very small and must be viewed through a microscope, such as bacteria and some algae.

SEE: BACTERIOLOGY, GERM

Microphone see Radio

Micropyle see Seed

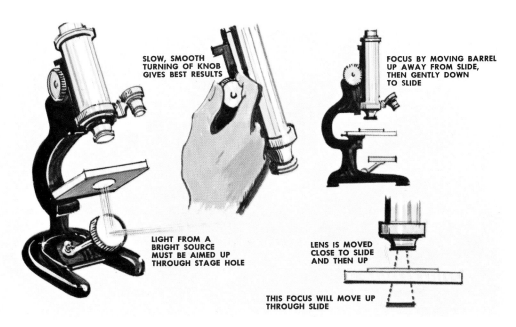

Adjusting the microscope for clear pictures

SLOW, SMOOTH TURNING OF KNOB GIVES BEST RESULTS

FOCUS BY MOVING BARREL UP AWAY FROM SLIDE, THEN GENTLY DOWN TO SLIDE

LIGHT FROM A BRIGHT SOURCE MUST BE AIMED UP THROUGH STAGE HOLE

LENS IS MOVED CLOSE TO SLIDE AND THEN UP

THIS FOCUS WILL MOVE UP THROUGH SLIDE

Microscope The microscope is an instrument used in magnifying objects too small to be seen by the naked eye. The word comes from *micro* meaning "small," and *scope,* "to see." The microscope is necessary in medical work for identifying bacteria, studying blood cells and tissue, and for other scientific research.

There are two kinds of microscopes, simple and compound. *Simple* microscopes are merely double convex lenses. A magnifying glass is a simple microscope. The *compound* microscope is what is meant when the term microscope is used. It has changed greatly since the first models of a few hundred years ago.

Basically, the compound microscope consists of one or more objective lenses (each is usually a system or group arranged to act as one lens), located near the object; and a second lens, an eyepiece. Objectives magnify various numbers of times, usually up to 90. The image is magnified further by the *eyepiece*. The eyepiece is located at the top of the tube, and the objective lenses at the bottom. The eyepiece commonly magnifies 10 times.

The specimen is placed on a slide which is held on the *stage,* a platform with an opening through which the light travels to

Parts of an optical microscope

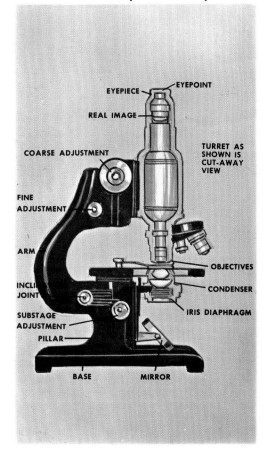

EYEPIECE

EYEPOINT

REAL IMAGE

COARSE ADJUSTMENT

TURRET AS SHOWN IS CUT-AWAY VIEW

FINE ADJUSTMENT

ARM

OBJECTIVES

INCLI JOINT

CONDENSER

SUBSTAGE ADJUSTMENT

IRIS DIAPHRAGM

PILLAR

BASE

MIRROR

✳ **THINGS TO DO**

MAKING MICROSCOPIC SPECIMEN SLIDES

Materials: microscopic slides, cover glasses, a jar of balsam, biological specimens

1 **Many objects of nature may be placed on the slide in a drop of water for temporary viewing, such as: wing of insect, fish scale, Elodea leaves, algae, molds, blood or other animal tissues.**

2 **For permanent slides, select small specimens which are semi-transparent. Cross sections of botanical life** **may be obtained by cutting thin slices with a razor blade or sharp knife. Place it on the center of the slide. Warm the balsam by placing the jar in a pan of hot water. Put one drop of balsam on top of the specimen and carefully place the cover glass over it so that no bubbles are permitted to form. The slide will dry overnight and be ready for observation under a microscope.**

the object and thence to the lenses. A mechanical stage has a device for controlled shifting of the slide.

The light source may be natural, with a mirror used to focus the rays toward the object. A *diaphragm* may control the light which enters the stage opening, as the intensity needed varies with the object, or power of magnification used. A condenser or lens may also be used at this point for light control. Microscopes regularly use electric lamps as a more dependable light source.

Holding the microscope together is the *arm* which connects the *base* and *stage* with the *tube*. It also acts as a convenient handle, housing the gears and controls for focusing —that is, adjusting the distance from object to object lens. There are usually two controls, coarse and fine. *Coarse adjustment* is always made first, after the objective lens has been lowered near the object. *Fine adjustment* should be used sparingly, since the gearing produces great power capable of

smashing lenses easily. When there is more than one objective, adjustment is made with the lowest power. Shifting to a higher power lens can usually be accomplished with little further focusing merely by turning the nosepiece on which the objective lenses are mounted.

Preparation of microscope slides involves several processes. Material must be fixed and preserved in a fixative that will not distort the tissues. Tissue water is removed by using a graded series of alcohol. Tissues are cleared (made transparent) with a clearing agent like xylol, then infiltrated with paraffin. Paraffin blocks of tissue are sectioned on a MICROTOME and the sections mounted on slides.

The slides now go through a five-step procedure. They are placed in xylol to remove the paraffin, dehydrated in a series of alcohol, stained to bring out structures, cleared once more in xylol, and covered with a thin glass cover slip cemented on the slide with a drop of Canadian balsam. D. J. I.

SEE ALSO: MICROSCOPE, ELECTRON

Microscope, electron The electron microscope is an instrument which permits scientists to see and photograph objects too small to be seen with an optical MICROSCOPE. The electron microscope uses beams of electrons in place of beams of light. It was developed by Albert Crewe at the University of Chicago's Enrico Fermi Institute and can magnify an object 7.5 million times. This permits observation and motion study of large atoms such as uranium in a molecule.

The human eye is a very fine non-magnifying OPTICAL INSTRUMENT. However, it cannot distinguish objects smaller than about $\frac{1}{4000}$ inch ($\frac{1}{1600}$ centimeter).

The limit of usefulness of an optical microscope is when the size of an object is so small that light waves can no longer define the object. Then the object becomes fuzzy. In the late 1920s, the French scientist Louis de Broglie, concurrent with an English physicist, George Thomson, determined that electrons have the properties of waves as well as some characteristics of particles. But the length of electron waves is much, much shorter than light waves. Making use of these facts, a German, Ruaka, made the first crude electron microscope. In 1937, a more refined one was built at the University of Toronto. This had a magnification of 7,000 times. Present-day electron microscopes have been improved until they produce very fine, direct images that can be further enlarged by photographic magnification.

The power of any enlarging instrument to form a distinct image of small details is its *resolving power,* or its *resolution.* Thus, the limit of resolution of an optical microscope is reached when objects cannot be distinguished because they are only slightly larger than the light waves reflected from them. The advantage of the electron microscope is that the electron waves are much shorter than the smallest light rays.

The resolution of electron microscopes is expressed in *angstroms* (Å), or *microns* (μ). An angstrom is about the diameter of the hydrogen atom, and the micron is one-thousandth of one millimeter. Electron microscopes achieve resolutions less than 100 Å.

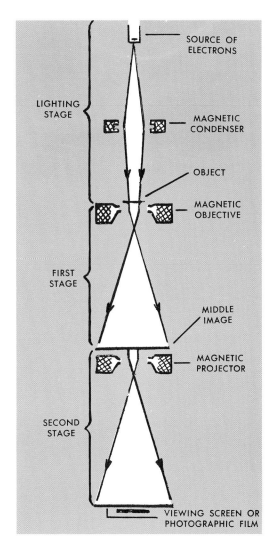

The electron microscope has a wide variety of uses. It has proved invaluable in the study of the atom and its complex structure. In chemistry and medicine it has revealed countless secrets of both organic and inorganic matter. The finest details of insect and plant life have been seen. In such areas as metallurgy and crystallography, old knowledge has been tremendously expanded. Scientists will learn much more about the world as the electron microscope is improved.

One scientist states that the electron microscope's ability to "see" within the nucleus of the atom "is another reason why physicists are eager to pile more and more electron-volts into their atom smashers." H. P. O.
SEE ALSO: ATOM, NUCLEAR SCIENCE

Microscopic measurements see Measurements

Microtome

Microtome (MY-kruh-tome) The microtome (*micro*—small; *tome*—cut) is an instrument used for cutting exceedingly thin slices of material to be used for microscope slides. With the microtome, otherwise opaque materials can be cut thin enough for thorough microscopic examination. Paper-thin slices or sections are produced. If the section is too thick, that is, having too many cells in depth, light cannot pass through, and the surface only, rather than interior detail, can be studied.

A microtome is a very precise instrument. It consists basically of a very sharp blade which can be adjusted to cut at various angles and at the thickness desired. Sections are measured in *microns* (1/1000 of a millimeter). The preparation, usually imbedded in PARAFFIN WAX, is mounted on a disk which advances with each slice for continuous sectioning, much as does a meat slicer in a grocery. Properly done, a continuous ribbon of sections appears like a series of paper dolls. One sample section or a series of sections may be examined.

The preparation of a specimen for sectioning is important for successful results. Materials can be made firm by freezing with carbon dioxide gas, and then sectioned. Mounting of slides and appropriate STAINING is done in final preparation for microscopic study. A second method of sectioning involves the dehydration of a specimen by a graded series of alcohol and xylol treatments. Impregnation by paraffin is then made. This leaves a preparation which can be stored quite indefinitely with no special difficulty. Sectioning and staining can be done as desired. Brittle sections, as of bone, are often imbedded in *celloidin* for support, but relatively thick sections result.

Examination of tissue for many purposes can be done by these methods. It is useful for the study of basic tissues and organs by students, for detecting abnormal cell conditions by doctors, and for general research purposes.   D. J. I.

SEE ALSO: HISTOLOGY, MICROSCOPE

Microwave see Electronics

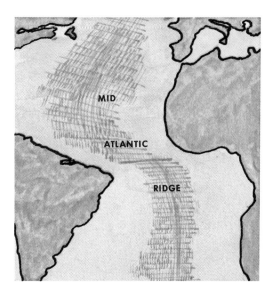

Mid-Atlantic Ridge The Mid-Atlantic Ridge is a chain of underwater volcanic mountains. They extend nearly the entire length of the Atlantic Ocean. Many of these peaks are above sea level and form ISLANDS. These peaks are formed by LAVA pouring out from cracks in the OCEAN floor.

The existence of the Mid-Atlantic Ridge was first discovered during the voyage of the *H.M.S. Challenger,* a wooden research vessel. Since that time, and especially after World War II, the use of SONAR and depth sounders have revealed that the sea floor consists of high mountains, PLATEAUS, deep TRENCHS, and large flat plains. The theory of PLATE TECTONICS states that oceanic ridges like the Mid-Atlantic Ridge are areas where molten rock from the Earth's interior flows out on to the surface. This process also results in sea-floor spreading and tends to push the continents away from each other.

There is a great deal of EARTHQUAKE and volcanic activity in the area around the Mid-Atlantic Ridge. The island of Iceland is part of the Ridge system, and volcanic eruptions, geysers, and earthquakes are common occurrences there.   P.P.S.

SEE ALSO: CONTINENTAL DRIFT, OCEANS

Midbrain This area of the brain is central and covered by the learning part of the brain (*cerebral hemispheres*). It partly controls seeing, hearing, some eye muscles, and muscle tone, in which 5 percent of the muscle fibers are always contracted.

SEE ALSO: NERVOUS SYSTEM

Midget A midget is an unusually small person. Midgets may be normal people in miniature, or they may have severe mental defects and physical deformities. Physicians speak of midgets as *dwarfs* and recognize three causes of most dwarfing.

If the PITUITARY gland does not produce enough growth-stimulating hormone, a person with normal intelligence and shape but smaller than normal size is produced. Pituitary dwarfs are rarely more than 55 inches (139.7 centimeters) tall.

If a person is born with a very inactive THYROID gland, he will be a midget known as a CRETIN. Cretins are mentally retarded and have a large protruding abdomen and short, thick limbs. Their faces are bloated and their tongues are thick and protruding.

Rickets, certain digestive disorders, childhood diabetes, and overactivity of the parathyroid glands, if untreated, can also cause dwarfing. Such midgets rarely live past adolescence because of the other disorders caused by these glandular deficiency diseases. J.K.L.

Midnight sun From the Arctic Circle to the North Pole, and the Antarctic Circle to the South Pole, are the "lands of the midnight sun." Here the sun will shine for 24 hours a day when it is the summer season for each of the Poles.

SEE ALSO: EARTH, EQUINOX

Migraine Migraine is a severe one-sided headache preceded by a disturbance of vision or "aura". Nausea and vomiting may follow.

Migraines seem to be due to constriction (narrowing) followed by dilation (widening) of an artery in the head on the affected side. Most headaches are not "migraines." A true migraine headache can be treated. Once the victim can recognize the "aura" (while the artery is still constricted), medications can be given to prevent the dilation, which often is the cause of the severe throbbing pain, nausea, and vomiting. Pain medications are sometimes useful too. E.S.S.

Reindeer migrate to the tundra for the summer

Migration Migration is the movement of animals from one place to another. Many people think the word "migration" refers only to the long seasonal journeys made by birds. However, many different kinds of animals, including humans, migrate. There are also different kinds of migration.

A pair of rabbits may have litters of three to six babies several times each year. If all the baby rabbits grew up and stayed close to their parents, and if they each had litters of their own which also grew up and stayed nearby, there soon would not be enough food in that neighborhood for all the rabbits. This is why most young animals move away from their parents as soon as they are able to take care of themselves. Gradually, the area in which these animals may be found spreads wider and wider. This is called *normal migration*. It is a slow type of migration which usually involves very short journeys over a period of many years.

Sometimes small animals, such as insects, snails, and frogs, are carried to new regions by floods or hurricane winds. Others, such as rats and lizards, may be carried away from their homes by strong ocean currents on small masses of tangled brush and earth washed out to sea. This is called *accidental migration*.

For hundreds of years people have helped

HOW DO ANIMALS MIGRATE?

Normal migration keeps animal concentrations low.

Sporadic migration due to overpopulation happens occasionally, as in lemmings.

Accidental migration takes animals far from their homes.

Animals migrate through man when people bring them on long journeys.

Periodic migration, like that of birds, happens at specific time periods.

animals migrate (move) from one place to another. This type of migration may be called *migration through man*. It has sometimes been done purposefully and sometimes has happened accidentally. Many animals, such as birds, dogs, cats, turtles, and cattle, have been carried by people from place to place as pets, or as sources of food. Others, such as rats, insects, and spiders, have been carried accidentally to new regions as stowaways.

Occasionally, animals that do not usually travel long distances will migrate in huge numbers. This *sporadic migration* happens only now and then and is usually the result of too many animals being born and living in one area. The occasional mass flights of locusts are examples of this type of migration.

The seasonal flights of birds are examples of *periodic migration*. This type of journey usually involves a return trip. It may be made as often as once each year, or as seldom as once in a lifetime. Some periodic migrations are long; some are short. Some involve large groups of animals; some involve only one or two. Most periodic migrations by animals are made for the purpose of breeding or feeding.

Long before birds lived on earth, animals (invertebrates) were making periodic migrations to find food, water of a certain temperature, or a safer place to lay their eggs. Horseshoe crabs have been making annual migrations for millions of years. Each spring they journey from the depths of the ocean to its sandy shores, where they lay their eggs.

Most fish migrate to shallow water in spring and back to deeper water in winter. They do this to find food and to find water of a certain temperature. Many fish migrate to spawn. Ocean salmon travel inland to rivers and streams to spawn. The baby fish then return to the ocean where they feed and grow until they, too, migrate inland.

Most birds migrate at least a short distance each spring and fall, either from North to South or from East to West. They do this to find food and desirable weather. Some of these migrations are very short but others are very long.

Birds may depend somewhat on landmarks along the way; however it is believed that they navigate chiefly by the sun during the day and by the stars at night. It is also thought that the earth's magnetism and a special "sixth sense" may play a part in guiding migrating birds. Migrating birds do not fly in straight lines but follow certain bands of skyway travel called *flyways*. There are four great flyways over North America:

the Atlantic Flyway, the Mississippi Flyway, the Central Flyway, and the Pacific Flyway.

Other animals which migrate long distances for feeding or breeding include northern fur seals, gray whales, caribou, and elephants. Animals cannot control their surroundings, so they must move to find conditions in which they can survive.

D. J. A.

SEE ALSO: BIRD

Migratory cells These are cells that move around in the body of an animal. Usually they "creep" like an AMEBA, putting out false feet or PSEUDOPODIA. They have many different jobs to do. Some digest while others remove waste, engulf unwanted solid particles, produce eggs or sperm, secrete, or help in clotting blood.

Some animals have a liquid-filled body cavity between the body wall and wall of the digestive tract. Often there are ameboid, or migratory, cells in the liquid of the cavity. In other animals, the cavity is filled with loose tissue. Ameboid cells may occur in spaces between tissue cells. When circulatory systems develop, many ameboid cells are in blood vessels. Others become part of organs like the LIVER, SPLEEN, and lymph nodes.

Ameboid cells are found among many phyla of animals. Many of these function in digestion or excretion. Ameboid cells in some animals may aid in clotting when the body is injured.

J. C. K.

Mildew Mildew is a plant that has no green coloring, or chlorophyll. It depends on living or dead plants for food. It has no roots, stems or leaves. It is a FUNGUS. It may live on plant products, such as cotton cloth.

The *powdery mildew* is a sac fungus or *ascomycete*. It gets its name from its white dusty appearance. It attacks lilac plants and some cereal grains. The hyphae grow down into the host plant. The powdery mildew spreads when *ascospores* break away from the spore cases.

Downy mildew is an alga-like fungus or *phycomycete*. It damages grapes, tobacco,

cabbage plants and some squash plants.

Dusting or spraying with sulfur helps to clear crops of this parasite. H. J. C.

Milk Milk is a liquid that comes from the breasts or udders of animals that nurse their young. These animals are called *mammals*. Although cow's milk is by far the most widely used, man has used milk from the mare, goat, ewe, camel, ass, zebra, reindeer, and llama. Cow's milk contains proteins, vitamins, fats, carbohydrates, and minerals. It has been considered almost a perfect food.

Because it is easily digested, milk is the chief food of infants. Adults, too, should have milk in order to get calcium and other needed vitamins. The milk of the Jersey and Guernsey cows is especially rich in fat. The milk of marine mammals, such as the seal and whale, is also very high in fat content. The milk of guinea pigs is rich in protein.

Skim milk, almost fat-free, is usually fortified with extra vitamins lost with the fat and is used in weight-control and cholesterol-control diets.

Federal, state, and local laws demand PASTEURIZATION of milk to destroy any germs that may be present in the milk.

Pesticide residue may be higher in human milk than in cow's milk. This is related to diet. A cow eats only plants whereas humans consume plants and other animals who have stored up pesticides. Their tissues accumulate a concentration of poisonous chemicals. Often breast-fed babies show a higher percentage of these contaminants than those on a formula of cow's milk.

Milk products include buttermilk, cheese, butter, cream, and ice cream. Milk by-products are cold-water paints, waterproof glues, face creams, buttons, combs, artificial wools, plastics, drugs, soft drinks, and insecticides. J.K.K.

SEE ALSO: DAIRY PRODUCTS, MAMMALIA

Milk sugar see Sugar

Milkweed see Seed dispersal, Wild flowers

The Milky Way galaxy as it appears in space

Milky Way The Milky Way is the band of hazy light that looks like a stream of spilled milk in the night sky. Through a telescope this light can be seen to be millions of stars. The Milky Way is a *galaxy,* which is a system of stars that move through the universe together. The SUN is one of the stars in the Milky Way.

There are probably over 100 billion stars in the Milky Way. There are also dark clouds or NEBULAE, which might be dust patches, gas clouds or dark bodies. Some areas of the Milky Way have brighter patches and streaks, which might be nebulae that reflect the light of neighboring stars. RADIO TELESCOPES have picked up noises which may one day explain what these cloudy areas really are.

Man's GALAXY is probably similar to other of the spiral galaxies that can be seen through telescopes. It is believed that from outside the Milky Way the stars would seem to form a giant pinwheel with five arms. This pinwheel is constantly spinning around in space. Some astronomers compare its appearance to a large whirling pancake.

The center of the Milky Way is thicker than the edges. Astronomers believe that the SOLAR SYSTEM is situated about half-way between the center and the edge of the Milky Way, on the inner edge of the fifth arm. Looking toward the center of the Milky Way, the band seems much brighter. A telescope pointed toward the center of the Milky Way shows a greater number of stars than can be seen toward the edge of the galaxy. The Milky Way is believed to be over 100,-000 light years wide.

There are many other galaxies in the universe that are similar to the Milky Way. Galaxies are sometimes called "island universes." A spiral galaxy can be seen in the constellation Andromeda. This is probably the nearest galaxy to the Milky Way. It is about two million light years away. C. L. K.
SEE ALSO: ASTRONOMY, INTERSTELLER COMMUNICATIONS, STAR, UNIVERSE

Millet Millet is a general term for a wide number of plants in the grass family. It is a cereal grain raised to feed humans and animals. Plants range in size from 1 foot (.3 meters) to 15 feet (4.57 meters) high. The flower head is a cluster of small blooms on one stalk. The grains are usually tiny and come in many colors.

Millet has a fibrous root system and a slender stem. In some species, the flower head may be an upright, thick spike and in others it will be a long, hanging spikelet of small flowers. The grain is rich in carbohydrates. Certain varieties can be made into nutritious bread flour.

Proso millet is the true millet. It is widely grown in Europe and Asia and now in the Great Plains of the United States. It is an excellent food to fatten up hogs in place of sorghum or corn.

Pearl millet grows up to 12 feet (3.66 meters) high and produces a white grain. *Japanese millet* has purplish grains. It is extremely popular in the Orient since several crops a year can be grown. H.J.C.

Millet

Millibar Millibars are number scales used to show AIR PRESSURE as recorded by barometers. The bar scale was adopted in 1939 by the United States Weather Bureau. Before this time, barometric pressure on the weather maps was shown in inches or millimeters of mercury at sea level.
SEE: BAROMETER, WEATHER MAP

Milligram see Measurement

Millikan's electronic charge (MILL-uh-kuhn) Between 1910 and 1916, Dr. Robert A. Millikan performed his now-classic "Oil Drop" experiment, which showed (1) that the charge of an electron is definite and not divisible, and (2) the size of this charge. Dr. Millikan received the Nobel Prize in physics in 1923 for his discoveries.

Millikan readapted a balance which equated the earth's pull (weight) against the pull created by an electric field on a charged body. He utilized Coulomb's law (unlike charges attract, and like charges repel).

Millikan used two horizontal plates, placed one above the other. The bottom plate was negatively charged; the top plate, positively charged. He sprayed a negatively charged fine droplet of oil between the plates. This droplet experienced an upward force toward the positively charged plate. If the oil drop's negative charge is called e, and the intensity of the field, controlled by the voltage between the two plates, is called E, the upward force on the drop is then eE. When eE equals the weight, W, of the drop, the drop will remain stationary between the two plates.

The weight of the drop and the intensity of the electric field can be determined by other means, and thus the charge e, on the drop can easily be calculated.

An important feature of the experiment was the possibility of changing the amount of charge which a drop could carry. This was accomplished by ionizing the air through which the drop falls by passing X-rays through the chamber. Hence, if a drop were rising, falling, or nearly balanced, its motion was changed when it acquired a measurable charge from another ion or electron.

Millikan was thus able to alter both the charge on the drop and the intensity of the field at will, keeping the drop under observation for quite a long period of time. The charge on a drop of liquid was never less than a certain amount; and, in fact, it was always once, or twice, or three times, or four times this amount. Millikan correctly assumed that this amount was the charge of one electron. Recent measurements show the charge of an electron to be 1.602192×10^{-19} coulombs.   M.B.C.

SEE ALSO: ELECTRICITY, CHARGED PARTICLES, IONIZATION

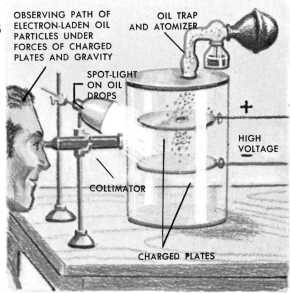

OBSERVING PATH OF ELECTRON-LADEN OIL PARTICLES UNDER FORCES OF CHARGED PLATES AND GRAVITY

OIL TRAP AND ATOMIZER

SPOT-LIGHT ON OIL DROPS

+

HIGH VOLTAGE

COLLIMATOR

CHARGED PLATES

Millikan's electrostatic oil drop charger

Millimeter see Measurement

Millipede A millipede is a worm-like animal with two pairs of legs on each body segment except for the first and last few segments. *Mill* means thousand and *pede* means feet. Millipedes do not have that many legs, but they may have over one hundred.

They are found in dark, moist places, in gardens, and in decaying food materials, upon which they live. They also feed on roots of living plants.

Millipedes protect themselves by curling so that the hard plates on their back cover them. They also have stink glands along the sides of their body.

Millipedes are in class Diplopoda, with more than 6,000 species. They average about 4 or 5 inches (10.16 or 12.7 centimeters) in length. They mate with legs that are hidden on the seventh segment of the male.   P.G.B.

Millipede   Buchsbaum

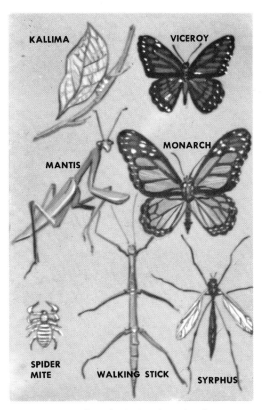

Examples of mimicry in animals

Mimicry (MIM-uh-kree) Mimicry is the resemblance of an animal to another animal or plant or to its surroundings. This resemblance, which often helps to protect the animal, is usually based on a similarity of color or structure.

Many examples of mimicry may be found among insects. The *dead leaf butterfly* of India, when resting, has the color and shape of a dead leaf and is therefore not disturbed by its enemies. People are often afraid of the harmless *hover fly* because it looks like a stinging wasp. The *viceroy* butterfly is rarely eaten by birds because it resembles the bad-tasting monarch butterfly. The *walking stick* looks just like a small twig. Spider mites that live among moss look just like part of the moss plant.

Many other animals also have protective coloring or structure. Young deer and some baby birds blend with their environment. The stripes of the tiger blend with the tall grass. Many nocturnal spiders are black and therefore difficult to see at night. Tree frogs are green. Arctic animals are often white. Protective coloring not only protects these animals from their enemies, but it also makes it possible for them to prey on other animals more easily. For example, the white fur of the polar bear, who has few enemies, enables it to approach its prey, the seal, unseen.

Animals do not plan a color or shape for themselves. Their protective coloring and structure is the result of selective evolution. Through the ages the animals with the most effective protective coloring and structure have survived the longest and therefore have been able to reproduce more of their kind. After many generations of breeding, more and more members of their species were born or hatched with the coloring and structure necessary for their survival.   D.J.A.
SEE ALSO: EVOLUTION, PROTECTIVE COLORATION

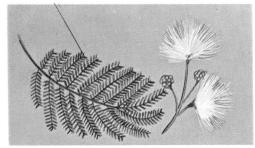

Mimosa

Mimosa (mih-MOH-suh) Mimosa are tropical American shrubs and trees of the PEA family. Of the many tropical species, only two are commonly raised in the United States. They are greenhouse plants but can be grown out-doors as annuals, in warm climates. In the tropics, mimosa is a PERENNIAL herb. Most mimosa plants are spiny, with attractive, feathery, sensitive leaves, and rose to purple clusters of flowers. The fruit is a flat pod, like a legume.

Mimosa pudica is sometimes called the *sensitive plant* because its leaves fold together and collapse when touched. *Mimosa spegazzini* also has slightly sensitive leaves. *Mimosa* comes from the Greek word meaning "mimic."   M. R. L.
SEE ALSO: LEGUME; PLANTS, TROPICAL

Mine, military see Weapons

Mineral Minerals are naturally occurring, inorganic substances of definite chemical composition. They make up the ROCKS of the Earth. Each mineral has its own specific physical and chemical characteristics. Table salt, gold, sulfur, and even clay are examples of the many different minerals.

Minerals may be either simple or complex substances. If a mineral is found to have only one kind of atom, it is a *simple mineral element*. But if a mineral is made up of two or more elements chemically united into one new substance, it is a *mineral compound*. To go one step further, ROCKS, to the geologist, are natural samples of one or more minerals, formed in the earth in a particular way. For example, CALCITE is crystalline calcium carbonate. But when calcium carbonate is deposited under oceans as a commonly dull, gray sediment, it is called *limestone*.

The *crystal shape* is important in identifying a mineral. As a mineral is being formed, the atoms or molecules of the mineral may arrange themselves in orderly patterns. These patterns then form flat-faced, regularly shaped solids which are known as *crystals*. The crystals of a given mineral may not always have the same shape. This property is called *habit*. The particular shape that a crystal assumes depends upon the conditions of its formation, and whether its growth was restricted or not.

The DIAMOND is an example of a valuable and beautiful mineral. It is the hardest known mineral. Thus it can be cut only with other diamonds. Ancient stonecutters found that by cutting and polishing a diamond in a certain way, light could be made to bounce from several sides inside the diamond before it reflected back to the eye, giving the typical sparkle. Other precious minerals are SAPPHIRE, EMERALD, and RUBY.

There is another group of minerals that may not have beauty, but are valuable in their own way. From these minerals, called *ores,* are obtained the metals necessary for modern economy. For example, *iron oxide*

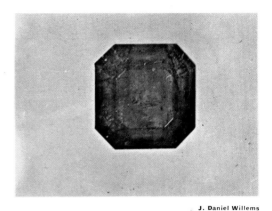

J. Daniel Willems
A cut emerald gem

J. Daniel Willems
A garnet crystal group

J. Daniel Willems
Quartz crystals

is found in some minerals. They are ores because man gets iron from them.

Over one hundred years ago large mineral deposits were discovered. In California, the mineral GOLD was discovered in 1849. This discovery helped settle the West. Ores of LEAD, SILVER, and gold were found in the Black Hills of South Dakota. Gold deposits occurring in great amounts were also found in Alaska and in the Yukon Territory of Canada. COPPER, ZINC, and MERCURY ores have

✳ THINGS TO DO

WHAT IS A MINERAL'S TRUE COLOR?

Materials: unglazed porcelain plate; samples of several minerals: pyrite, galena, hematite, sphalerite

1 Take the minerals and scratch each one across the porcelain plate.
2 What colors are the streaks? Are they the same color as the minerals? The test shows a mineral's true color.

✳ THINGS TO DO

DO ANIMALS HAVE MINERALS?

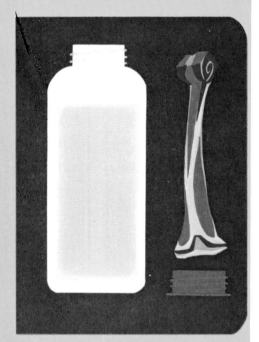

1 Clean all the muscle from a chicken bone. Put the bone into a covered jar of strong vinegar solution for several days.
2 Remove it and you will find that it is extremely flexible. The minerals have been removed by the acid.
3 One of the main functions of minerals in the skeleton is to make it strong and durable.

also been located and heavily mined in several northern and western states.

A large proportion of the predictable mineral resources have been located, and a large number have already been used in the industrial expansion of the nation. Some metals that are found in only small amounts, such as tin, must be imported from other countries.

Because man uses such huge quantities of these valuable minerals, he is always trying to find new deposits. One of the new methods of prospecting for mineral deposits uses airplane or spacecraft photography. By using these new methods, the geologist can see in greater detail the physical structure of the land. This tells the geologist the specific processes that form the land and it provides valuable clues to the types of minerals that may be found there.

Oil (petroleum) is an important earth material that is used for fuel. Petroleum occurs mainly in *sedimentary* rocks. It is generally believed that petroleum is formed from oil-bearing or oil-forming plants and animals. Large accumulations of such organic remains have been deposited in ancient, shallow, inland seas as well as in shallow coastal areas. Sometimes rock layers containing oil form in an upfold (*anticline*). Then the oil is always found at the top of the anticline.

Probably one of the most remarkable discoveries of valuable minerals occurred in 1892. It is recorded that Pete Helmquist, a handyman in a logging camp, was digging a well in the Mesabi Mountain Range near Hibbing, Minnesota; after digging through 6 feet (1.8 meters) of CLAY, his shovel hit a

Tourmaline crystals showing many colors because of trace mineral impurities

J. Daniel Willems

reddish substance. This substance was almost too heavy for him to lift. Great excitement resulted, and prompted the loggers to send for a mining engineer. This mining engineer was Frank Hibbing, who took samples of ore and found it to be the richest iron ore yet discovered. Pete Helmquist's well was the starting point for the world's largest mine.

Today, the high-grade ore of the Mesabi Range is running out. However, new, rich iron ore deposits have been discovered in Canada and South America. Also, by the new Taconite process, mining chemists have learned how to get iron from Minnesota ores formerly considered too low-grade to use.

There are still vast, remote areas in the world that may yield productive deposits of minerals. It is the task of the geologists and minerologists to locate mineral wealth to replace the depleted stocks. It is also the task of the chemist to find new ways to reclaim used minerals and discover new substitutes or synthetics that will take the place of depleted minerals.   V.V.N.

SEE ALSO: CRYSTAL, GEM, HARDNESS SCALE, METAL, MINERALOGY, NATURAL RESOURCES

Mineral water Mineral water is water which has a higher content of dissolved minerals or gas than ordinary WATER. All water contains some dissolved minerals.

The composition of mineral water depends on the kind of rock and soil through which it has passed. Some of the chemicals likely to be in it are compounds of silicon, calcium, magnesium, sodium, potassium, iron, and manganese, and hydrogen sulfide gas. Mineral water in different places has different tastes and temperatures. It can be cold or hot, alkaline, salty, carbonated; or it can have a strong odor and taste of sulfide.

Drinking mineral water is thought to benefit the body. There are over 9,000 mineral springs in North America, in over 3,000 places.   E.R.B.

Mineralogy (minn-er-AHL-uh-jee) Mineralogy is the scientific study, identification, and classification of minerals. Minerals make up the rocks of the crust of the Earth. Identification of minerals may be made in three different ways: by their physical characteristics; by their chemical composition; or by optical means. A mineralogist usually will first try to identify an unknown mineral by looking at physical characteristics of the mineral.

Mineralogy is one of the very old sciences. During the STONE AGE, man knew about, and used, minerals. By the Bronze Age, man was familiar with the process of smelting, to obtain metal from natural compounds.

With the invention and development of new techniques of mineral study and the rapid discovery of new minerals, the accumulating data on the subject of minerals and mineralogy has grown to tremendous proportions. At present, there are many specialized classifications, or fields, of mineralogy, some of which are sub-classified further. The four principal branches of this science, however, are crystallography, physical mineralogy, optical mineralogy, and chemical mineralogy.

CRYSTALLOGRAPHY

Crystallography is dependent upon the field of solid GEOMETRY, and studies the form of minerals. Almost all minerals are solid, and usually crystalline. Each CRYSTAL is internally arranged in a precise geometric pattern. A crystal is a solid bounded by natural plane surfaces called "faces." A crystal may be so completely distinctive in appearance that this feature alone is sufficient for identification of the mineral. Many other physical properties used for identifying minerals are dependent upon the crystal structure. Crystallography includes the description and classification of crystals, and also deals with the relationship of the forms of crystals with their atomic structure and properties.

Crystals are studied according to crystal systems, based on imaginary axes of refer-

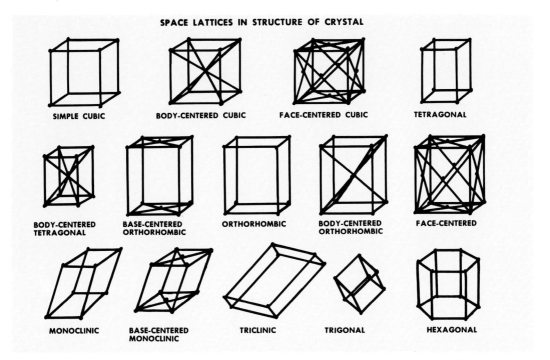

SPACE LATTICES IN STRUCTURE OF CRYSTAL

SIMPLE CUBIC · BODY-CENTERED CUBIC · FACE-CENTERED CUBIC · TETRAGONAL

BODY-CENTERED TETRAGONAL · BASE-CENTERED ORTHORHOMBIC · ORTHORHOMBIC · BODY-CENTERED ORTHORHOMBIC · FACE-CENTERED

MONOCLINIC · BASE-CENTERED MONOCLINIC · TRICLINIC · TRIGONAL · HEXAGONAL

ence; classes of symmetry, including planes, axes, and center symmetry; and crystal faces.

PHYSICAL MINERALOGY

Physical mineralogy deals with the physical properties and characteristics of minerals. Since most minerals can be identified by physical properties alone, this branch is a most important tool. This classification includes:

Hardness: The property of a mineral that makes it resist scratching or abrasion is one of many physical characteristics used in identification. A harder mineral will scratch a softer one. A scale of standard hardness (*Moh scale*) places all minerals within a range of 1 to 10. Talc, the softest, is assigned number 1 and diamond, the hardest, is assigned number 10.

Cleavage: The splitting of a mineral along some crystal plane is called *cleavage*. Not all minerals show cleavage. The quality of cleavage is termed perfect, good, indistinct, and imperfect.

Fracture: Separation of a mineral other than by cleavage is called *fracture*. After fracture, the surface may be even, splintery, hackly, rough, smooth, or conchoidal (shell-like).

Luster: Luster is concerned with the degree and kind of brilliance. The two major divisions are *metallic* and *nonmetallic*.

Mineral compounds such as GALENA and PYRITE which look like metal elements, and metals such as COPPER are called metallic. These types of luster are described as iron black, steel grey, tin white, or golden yellow. Some minerals are *submetallic;* and all others are nonmetallic in luster, such as quartz, sphalerite, and DIAMOND. Nonmetallic lusters may be silky, chatoyant, pearly, resinous, waxy, greasy, or pitchy.

Color: If a mineral has a constant color, it is termed *idiochromatic*. Copper minerals *azurite* and *malachite* are always blue and green, respectively. *Allochromatic* refers to minerals with variable colors. QUARTZ, for example, comes in a large variety of hues. A *play of colors* refers to internal flashes of color, such as in the precious opal. If it is somewhat milky, it is called *opalescent*. The degree of transparency is designated as opaque, translucent, or transparent.

Streak: If a mineral is ground to a fine powder and rubbed on unglazed white porcelain, it leaves a streak or color that may be different from its original. If a mineral is harder than the streak plate, it is said to have a colorless streak.

Specific gravity: The SPECIFIC GRAVITY of a mineral is the ratio of its weight to the weight of an equal volume of water (at 39.2° F or 4° C).

The degree of magnetism, the electrical

properties (degree of conductivity), and the structure (*amorphous*—devoid of crystal faces—or *crystalline*) of minerals are further identifying characteristics. Taste, smell and touch, as well as the ELASTICITY, malleability, tenacity and ductility, are also characteristics which help in identifying the mineral.

OPTICAL MINERALOGY

Crushed mineral fragments or thin sections may be studied microscopically. Characteristic shapes, cleavage cracks, colors, and other details may be seen with ordinary light; however, plane-polarized light may be used for measuring indices of refraction. Often, these properties may be sufficient to identify the mineral. Optical methods are especially helpful in studying twin crystals.

CHEMICAL MINERALOGY

This branch of mineralogy studies the chemical composition of minerals, and relies heavily upon the field of analytical CHEMISTRY to give the methods used in determining composition.

Minerals are either ELEMENTS or chemical COMPOUNDS, and they can be analyzed and their formula calculated in the same manner as other chemical substances, that is, by standard procedures of quantitative analysis.

In obtaining the composition and formula of a supposed new mineral, a detailed and accurate analysis is first prepared. Then, the percentages of these elements are divided by the atomic weights. A simple ratio of whole numbers can thus be obtained and the chemical formula can then be expressed.

In the case of *microcline feldspar,* composed of potassium (K), aluminum (Al), Silicon (Si) and oxygen (O), an analysis showed a ratio of percentages divided by the atomic weights to be $1:1:3:8$ respectively. Therefore, the formula of this mineral is $KAlSi_3O_8$.

For the purposes of identification, qualitative analysis of minerals is now widely employed. Three common procedures of qualitative analysis for analyzing minerals are wet chemical tests, blowpipe tests, and spectroscopic analyses.

While a few of the elements, such as nitrogen, are rarely found in mineral form, minerals are the chief source for a great many chemical elements.

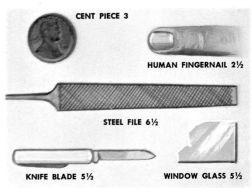

The above items can serve as a handy pocket hardness scale test of minerals

DESCRIPTIVE MINERALOGY

Descriptive mineralogy organizes the results of the studies of minerals, and classifies the different species so that the related minerals will be grouped together.

DETERMINATIVE MINERALOGY

Determinative mineralogy is concerned with identifying minerals. Known minerals may be identified by simple methods such as sight, if some obvious feature exists. Newly discovered minerals are more difficult to classify. Determinative mineralogy makes use of tables and charts with minerals arranged in a systematic order.   D. L. D.
SEE ALSO: HARDNESS SCALE, METAL, MINERALS

Mining see Coal, Metal, Mineral

Mink see Weasel

Minnow A minnow is a very small, fresh water fish. The golden shiner, roach, small carp, dace, and gambusia are some of the fishes generally known as minnows. They are the natural food of many larger fish and are generally used as a good bait by fishermen.

Some decorative types of minnows are used in home aquariums. Minnows, especially the gambusia, which bears living young, are valuable in mosquito control. The young fish devour mosquito larvae.   M. R. L.

Common shiner, a minnow
Chicago Natural History Museum

Mint

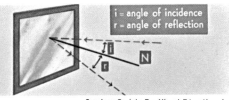

The boy would have to move to the right to see the reflection of the apple because the angles do not cross the normal position (N)

Mint

Mint Mint is the name of a large family of plants. Some are catnip, thyme, bee balm, lavender, peppermint, spearmint, sage, rosemary, and marjoram. These plants are grown all over the world and have many uses, especially in flavorings.

The common variety of mint that grows in gardens is a hardy PERENNIAL with square stems, creeping roots, and light purple blossoms. The fragrant leaves grow in pairs, one on each side of the stem. Mint is a favorite cooking herb and is used in sauces, iced tea, vegetables, and jellies.   J. K. K.
SEE ALSO: CATNIP, MARJORAM, PEPPERMINT, ROSEMARY, SAGE, SPEARMINT, THYME.

Minuteman missile see Missile

Miocene see Cenozoic Era, Geologic time table

Mirage (mih-RAHZH) A mirage is a reflection caused by bending LIGHT rays. When riding along a highway, one may sometimes see a reflection ahead which looks like a distant pool of water. People traveling across a desert will occasionally see what appears to be a distant lake, only to find it disappear as they move toward it. These reflections are mirages caused by a layer of dense warm air near the surface of the earth. Light rays bend when they pass through substances of different densities. The light rays from the sky are reflected toward one's line of vision by the dense warm air near the ground; so what one sees is not water, but a reflection of the sky.

Mirror A mirror is any smooth surface which reflects more light rays than it absorbs. All mirrors absorb some light, but the more highly polished they are, the more they will reflect. Even a highly polished sheet of glass will act as a mirror, to an extent, although it allows most of the rays to pass through. The condition of being *opaque* and the smoothness of surface determine the quality of REFLECTION. Good mirrors are made of polished glass with a silvery back surface.

The angle between a light ray striking a mirror and the normal (perpendicular) to the mirror is the *angle of incidence*. The angle between the normal and the ray reflecting off the mirror is the *angle of reflection*. These two angles are always equal.

Mirrors are of three kinds: Plane, or flat, concave, and convex. A *concave* mirror is one whose surface is like the inside of a hollow ball. It will reflect a larger or smaller image depending on the object's distance from it. If the object is further away, the image will appear upside down. A convex mirror always shows an image smaller than the object. Concave mirrors are used in reflecting telescopes.   D. J. I.
SEE ALSO: LENS, MAN-MADE; LIGHT; OPAQUE; TELESCOPE

A mirage appears in a straight line of sight on the pavement. The bright sky is the source of light which changes direction at the boundary of warm surface air and cooler upper air. It appears to be water since water is detected by its reflection

COOL AIR LAYER

HOT AIR LA

The rocket Saturn V had a more peaceful purpose than missiles. Instead of a warhead, its payload was an Apollo spacecraft.

Missile (MISS-uhl) A missile is a self-propelled projectile. As a weapon system, it replaces, in part, artillery and the bomber. It is an automatic system, equipped with guidance and control. Missiles are generally grouped as Surface-to-Surface Missiles (SSM), Air-to-Air Missiles (AAM), Surface-to-Air Missiles (SAM), Air-to-Surface Missiles (ASM).

THE RANGE OF MISSILES

The three most important of these groups are the SSM, the SAM, and the ASM. The SSMs are divided into categories according to range. The short range ones can travel 100 nautical miles (185 kilometers). The medium range go from 300 to 1,000 nautical miles (550 to 1,850 kilometers). The intermediate range go 1,000 to 3,000 nautical miles (1,850 to 5,550 kilometers), and intercontinental range goes from 5,000 to 8,000 nautical miles (9,300 to 14,800 kilometers).

The United States and Canada are in joint defense of North America. Canada supplies air and sea support, while the United States employs a *triad* defense—missiles that can be launched from land, sea, or air.

MISSILE COMPONENTS

Common missile components are the warhead, the guidance and control system, the propellant system, and the engine system. The *warhead* comprises the bomb, auxiliary equipment to set the bomb off, and external structure.

The *guidance* and *control system* consists of the guidance system, the autopilot and the guidance control system. This system can be compared with the human system which it resembles (page 1074). The heart, or vital component, of the system is the *autopilot,* since the system must first of all be capable of a stable posture to insure stability of flight in motion. Only then can the guid-

The Hawk surface-to-air missile.

U.S. Air Force

ance system exercise control in "telling" the autopilot where to make the missile go. Guidance signals would be useless to a tumbling missile. The guidance system steers; the autopilot stabilizes the missile in compliance with the steering commands.

The guidance system formulates the steering commands as the result of information which is evaluated in a COMPUTER. Basic and predictable information comes from the *programmer,* specifying a predetermined sequence of events which the missile must follow. No more would be required if everything inside the missile would work with perfect accuracy and if everything on the outside (e.g. winds, gusts, etc.) were perfectly predictable. Since this is not the case, additional information is required, either from the ground (radio signals) or from sensors on board (gyroscopes and accelerometers), which permit the missile to check the accuracy of its motion by evaluating error signals in the computer. In the *radio guidance system* this computer is on the ground, and the corrective signal is radio-transmitted to the missile. In the *inertial guidance system* the computer is on board. Either way, the combined information from programmer and error signals results in steering signals to the autopilot, which now issues signals (commands) which the servo-actuators can "understand" or act upon.

First, the signal strength must be increased and, where necessary, the original direct current must be transformed into an alternating current. All this happens in a combination of the tube amplifier with either oscillating switch (chopper) or vibrator, or

in a magnetic amplifier with rectifier. Electrical relays (SOLENOID or pneumatic) and valves (controllers) respond to these *servo-control* signals and they in turn control the amount of "muscle force" to be applied by the actuators in order to assure smooth corrections and avoid violent movements. The *servo-actuators,* activated by the controllers, deflect aerodynamic control surfaces, or rocket engines, in such a manner as to change altitude and course of the missile according to direction by the autopilot. By measuring the actual corrective action taken (*feedback*), the autopilot determines whether its commands have been carried out accurately or whether further corrections are necessary. Then the control loop is closed.

Nearly all missiles are powered by rocket engines. The *liquid propellant* rocket has separate tanks from which the fuel and oxidizer is pumped to the engine's combustion chamber. *Solid fuel* engines have the propellant solidified in the combustion chamber. The liquid propellants are much more difficult to handle, but generally have a higher *specific impulse* or thrust factor than solid fuel. Jet engines power a few missiles, but most use rocket propulsion systems. The *Minuteman* ICBM (solid fuel) and the cruise missile (liquid fuel) are rocket propelled.

While under development, missiles carry a large amount of on-board instrumentation, measuring the operation of their various components. This is necessary first in order to find the cause of missile flight failures which always end in destruction of the vehicle, and second, to monitor the performance of specific vehicle components and to determine the flight performance. Because of this second reason, even operational missiles carry a limited amount of on-board instrumentation. These measurements monitor the guidance and control system, tank pressures, propellent motion ("sloshing"), engine pumps and turbine, thrust chamber motion, pressures and temperatures in electronic packages, hydraulic and pneumatic pressures, skin temperatures, and structural stresses. The data is transmitted to ground stations.

LAUNCHING BASE

All missiles must have a suitable means of launching in order to become an effective weapon. Some missiles are fired from aircraft, while others utilize a wide variety of fixed

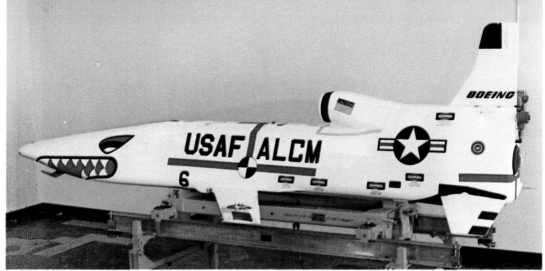

One of two designs for the recently developed cruise missile.

SOME TYPICAL U.S. MISSILES

Minuteman—this is a three-stage, solid-fueled ICBM, launched from an underground silo. Its inertial guidance system can direct it to targets over 8,000 miles (12,900 kilometers) away.

Titan—a military launch vehicle, liquid-fueled, with two booster rockets. Its lift-off thrust is 2.4 million pounds (10.7 kilonewtons).

Poseidon—a solid-fueled missile also designed to be launched from a submarine. Its range is 2,500 nautical miles (2,800 to 4,600 kilometers).

Trident—this solid-fueled missile will replace the Poseidon missile. Its range is greater, a distance of 4,000 nautical miles (7,400 kilometers).

Cruise missile—a liquid-fueled missile with a inertial and terrain comparison guidance system. It follows the earth's contours at low altitudes to avoid radar detection. It flies at the speed of sound. It can be launched either from the air or from a submarine.

Pershing—a solid-fueled missile with an inertial guidance system. This missile is launched from an erector and is a long-range, surface-to-surface weapon.

Dragon—this solid-fueled missile has an infrared (heat-seeking) guidance system. It weighs 6½ pounds (2.9 kilograms) and is launched by one man, rather like a bazooka.

Falcon—an air-to-air, solid-fueled missile launched from a fighter aircraft. It has an infrared (heat-seeking) guidance system.

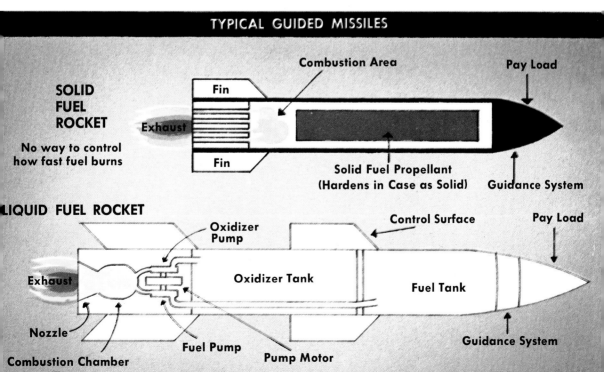

TYPICAL GUIDED MISSILES

SOLID FUEL ROCKET

No way to control how fast fuel burns

Fin

Fin

Exhaust

Combustion Area

Pay Load

Solid Fuel Propellant (Hardens in Case as Solid)

Guidance System

LIQUID FUEL ROCKET

Oxidizer Pump

Control Surface

Pay Load

Exhaust

Oxidizer Tank

Fuel Tank

Nozzle

Combustion Chamber

Fuel Pump

Pump Motor

Guidance System

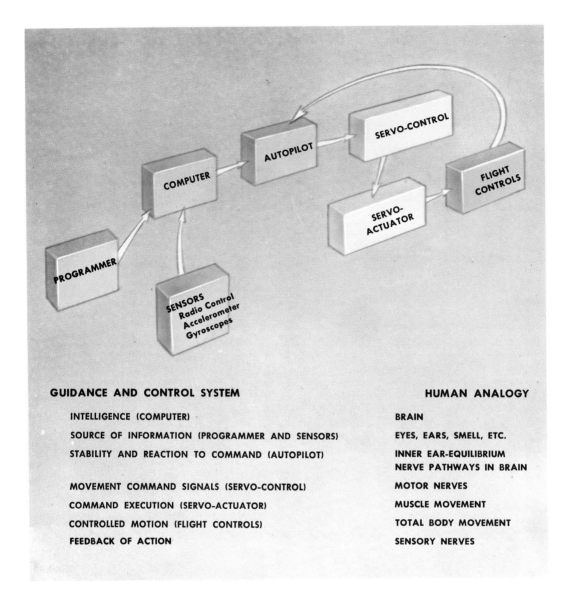

GUIDANCE AND CONTROL SYSTEM · · · · · · · · · · · HUMAN ANALOGY

INTELLIGENCE (COMPUTER) · BRAIN

SOURCE OF INFORMATION (PROGRAMMER AND SENSORS) · · · · EYES, EARS, SMELL, ETC.

STABILITY AND REACTION TO COMMAND (AUTOPILOT) · · · · · · INNER EAR-EQUILIBRIUM
· NERVE PATHWAYS IN BRAIN

MOVEMENT COMMAND SIGNALS (SERVO-CONTROL) · · · · · · · MOTOR NERVES

COMMAND EXECUTION (SERVO-ACTUATOR) · · · · · · · · · · · · MUSCLE MOVEMENT

CONTROLLED MOTION (FLIGHT CONTROLS) · · · · · · · · · · · · · TOTAL BODY MOVEMENT

FEEDBACK OF ACTION · SENSORY NERVES

and mobile launch platforms. The larger missiles require extensive facilities, which include the launch complex, storage and repair facilities, and checkout and flight data systems.

As a major weapon system, a rapid launch capability with maximum protection from enemy attack is a prime concern. The army utilizes the mobility of trucks and trailers to keep the exact location of its *Pershing* (MRBM) missiles secret. Navy missile-carrying submarines are constantly cruising the oceans. Complex computers on board provide exact predetermined target coordinates and other launch data to their *Polaris* and *Poseidon* missile guidance systems.

The Strategic Air Command's Intercontinental Ballistic Missiles (ICBM) are deployed at hundreds of blast-proof or *hardened* underground launch sites called *silos*. These missile bases are constantly manned, and undergo frequent readiness checks. An elaborate communications system links the control center with each silo for an almost immediate firing of the ICBMS. The liquid-fueled *Atlas* has been replaced by the three-stage, solid-fuel *Minuteman*, which has a simpler storage and launch capability. This missile is about 60 feet (18.3 meters) tall, and weighs about 70,000 pounds (31,752 kilograms). The advanced *Titan II* is still operational.

The breakup of the Soviet Union in 1991 and the end of the Cold War has, at least temporarily, shifted world attention away from

Courtesy Society For Visual Education, Inc.
Mistletoe

ICBMs. But a brief war in 1991 showed clearly the devastating effect smaller missiles can have in warfare.

THE MISSILES OF DESERT STORM

Some people described the U.S. Army's *Patriot* antimissile missile as the hero of the 1991 Gulf War. The Patriot was first built in 1979 but was untested in actual warfare until Jan. 18, 1991. During Desert Storm, the little missile proved capable of destroying Iraqi *Scud* missiles in flight. The Patriot's electronic launch system determined the quantity and types of targets. RADAR systems on the ground and in the missiles themselves tracked the targets until the targets were destroyed. At the same time, computer systems determined in a split second whether additional missiles needed to be launched.

Tomahawk cruise missiles were the first U.S. weapons used to attack Iraqi forces during pre-dawn raids. Capable of carrying a 1,000-pound (454-kilogram) warhead up to 800 miles (nearly 1,300 kilometers), Tomahawks often flew close to the ground. Cruise missiles are guided by onboard computers that follow electronic maps of the terrain the missile is programmed to fly over. On the first day of the war, the U.S.S. *Wisconsin* coordinated the launching of 45 cruise missiles from six different warships in the Red Sea and the Persian Gulf. Military experts say that cruise missiles can strike within 30 feet (9 meters) of their targets.

The High-Speed Anti-Radiation Missile (HARM) is designed to destroy enemy radar equipment. HARM warheads carry thousands of little steel cubes which, when the warhead explodes, strike and damage radar antennas. In the early stages of the war, many Iraqi radar operators were forced to turn off their equipment as the only defense against HARMs.

Another type of Desert Storm weapon, called a smart bomb, was actually a type of guided missile. Some smart bombs had television cameras mounted in their payloads. The success of high-tech weapons, including missiles, during Desert Storm was considered by many a vindication for trillions of dollars spent on controversial defense hardware by the administration of U.S. President Ronald Reagan.   K.A.E./J.H.

SEE ALSO: AIRCRAFT, ASTRONAUTICS, AUTOMATION, JET PROPULSION, PROJECTILES, ROCKET, ROCKET ENGINES, ROCKET PROPELLANTS, SPACE VEHICLES

Mistletoe (MISS-uhl-toh) Mistletoe is a parasite. It attaches itself to trees such as the apple tree, willow, maple, mesquite, poplar, hawthorn, sycamore, locust and fir. It gets its food from the trees to which it clings. Mistletoe has small, smooth evergreen leaves and tiny yellow flowers which bloom in February and March. The fruit is a white, waxy berry about ¼ inch (0.6 centimeter) in diameter.

Mistral The mistral is a cold, dry WIND which blows down from the snow-covered Alps, to the southern coast of France. It blows from a high pressure area to one of low pressure.
SEE: CLIMATE, WEATHER

Mite Some mites live on the outside of animals and plants. Others are free-living. They are very small and have sucking mouthparts.

Mites and ticks are both grouped into order *Acarina,* the larger species being called *ticks.* A mite or tick is not an insect; a mite has only two body divisions, a *cephalothorax* and an *abdomen.* Unlike the six-legged insects, mites as adults have eight legs; though nymph stages may possess six legs at first.

Chiggers are the young or larvae of red mites. They have six legs instead of the eight found in the adult. Most lack eyes, and the body is fused into one piece. They will feed upon the blood of humans. They secrete an irritating juice as they bite holes in the skin. The itching and red blotches will last for several days.   J.C.K./H.J.C.

Mitochondria see Cells

Red harvest mite (left), chicken mite (right)

Simple cell division

Mitosis and meiosis (my-TOE-siss and my-OH-siss) The purpose of mitosis and meiosis is to divide nuclear material between two cells. Nuclear material is made of *chromatin.* Most of chromatin is a NUCLEIC ACID, DNA. Just before mitosis, or division, MOLECULES of DNA are copied so that two sets of chromatin, with its DNA molecules, are in one nucleus. In mitosis, each of the new cells receives one complete set of DNA molecules.

Through DNA, nuclei control work done in a cell and inheritance of cell structures. If part of a nucleus were missing, the cell could not do its work. Any missing *cytoplasm* (the part of living material surrounding the nucleus) can be replaced by the nucleus.

Mitosis is necessary for replacement of old cells and for reproduction (*binary fission*) among lower plants and animals.

Meiosis in animals occurs only in the formation of *germ cells* (eggs or sperm). In plants it occurs when SPORES are formed. Living cells have a constant number of paired CHROMOSOMES in their nuclei. In meiosis, the number of chromosomes is halved. One of each pair enters a daughter cell. When eggs and sperm unite, the full number of chromosomes is restored. Spores form a plant (*gametophyte*) with half the number of chromosomes.

PROCESS OF MITOSIS

In between divisions, the cell is said to be in *interphase.* At this time it seems to be resting but is very active metabolically in that many chemical and physical changes are taking place at the molecular level.

Chromosomes are in the form of a network of fine threads called the *linin* network. Threads are composed of PROTEIN and DNA. The kind of protein depends on the species of plant or animal but often it is *histone.* As far as is known, the protein has no genetic or controlling function, so is commonly disregarded. What happens to the DNA is important. Also present are one or more *nucleoli.* Their number is constant for a given kind of plant or animal and they store DNA.

During interphase, DNA molecules come apart in the center. Each half adds (*synthesizes*) another half. At the end of the stage, chromatin threads are double, or *bivalent.*

Interphase is followed by the *prophase* stage. The chromatin threads gradually coil around each other and condense into solid rodlike bodies. These darkly stained bodies are chromosomes. Each is bivalent due to the activity in interphase. Located on each chromosome is a non-genetic, undivided particle called a *centromere.* Each part of the bivalent thread is called a *chromatid.*

Along with chromosome condensation, the nucleolus becomes indistinct and finally disappears. The nuclear membrane breaks up. In animal cells a *centriole,* or particle outside the nucleus, divides and one centriole moves to the other side of the center of the cell. As they separate, a spindle of clear fibers forms in the cytoplasm between them. Radiating out from each centriole, at the poles of the spindle, are fibers or *astral rays.* The rays around each centriole make up an *aster.* In plants, spindles form without centrioles or asters, and form before the nuclear membrane breaks up.

In late prophase, or *prometaphase,* chromosomes clump in the center of the cell while the spindle finishes forming. Spindle fibers are composed of 90 percent protein, 5 percent ribonucleic acid (RNA) and some *lipid* or fat. Fibers are elastic and gelatinous. Some go from pole to pole while others go to the center of the spindle and attach to the centromere regions of chromosomes.

Prophase lasts from one to several hours and is followed by *metaphase,* which is usually shorter. The spindle has formed around the chromosomes and some of the fibers are attached to the centromeres of the chromosomes. Fibers guide the chromosomes to the center of the spindle, the *equatorial plate.* The single centromeres holding the bivalent chromosomes together now divide.

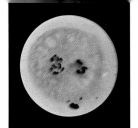

Mitosis in a fertilized egg, zygote, starts with two masses of nuclear chromatin— from egg and sperm (magnified 750 times)

During pro-metaphase, the chromosomes become much shorter and thicker, begin to pair up, and take on identifiable shapes

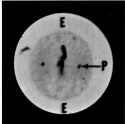

In metaphase, the chromosomes line up on the equatorial plate (from E to E). At each pole is a centriole (P) radiating the aster

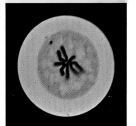

Metaphase seen from the polar view shows the chromosomes more clearly. There are both U-shaped and bent kinds that pair up

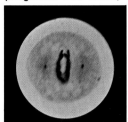

In early anaphase, chromosomes have separated, making nuclear material for two cells. They start to form two groups

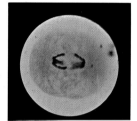

During anaphase, the chromosomes have formed two separate groups. They are drawn toward the centrioles and asters

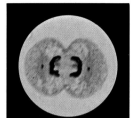

During telophase, the cell membrane begins to pinch in, dividing the cytoplasm into two masses, forming separate cells

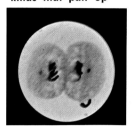

Photo-micrographs by National Teaching Aids, Inc.

The separation becomes complete in late telophase. Cell has nuclear material from both parents. Cells rest during interphase

The important aspect of meiosis is the reduction in the number of chromosomes

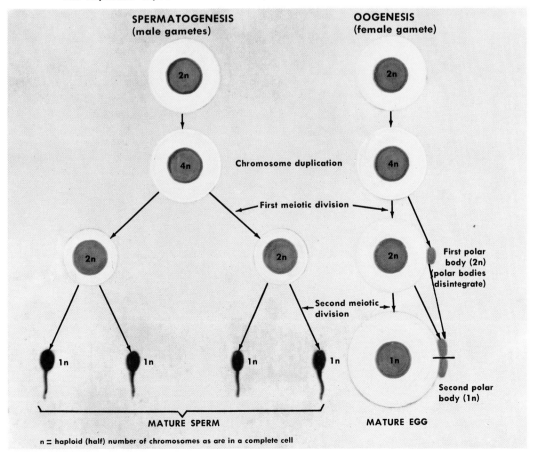

SPERMATOGENESIS (male gametes)

OOGENESIS (female gamete)

2n

2n

4n

Chromosome duplication

4n

First meiotic division

2n

2n

2n

First polar body (2n) (polar bodies disintegrate)

Second meiotic division

1n

1n

1n

1n

1n

Second polar body (1n)

MATURE SPERM

MATURE EGG

n = haploid (half) number of chromosomes as are in a complete cell

When chromosomes begin to migrate toward the poles the *anaphase* stage begins. After division of the centromere, each chromatid is called a *daughter chromosome*. The part of the chromosome going first along the fiber toward the poles is the centromere. The shape of the moving chromosome depends on the position of the centromere. For example, central positions produce V-shaped chromosomes. Anaphase is over when all daughter chromosomes reach the poles.

The final stage of mitosis is called *telophase*.This stage is one of cellular reorganization, ending with the formation of another interphase cell. In general, telophase is the opposite of prophase, and it lasts about the same length of time. The chromosomes uncoil and form a linin network, the nucleolus reappears (the mechanics of its disappearance and reappearance are unknown), and the nuclear membrane reforms. In animals the cytoplasm cleaves, cutting the cell into two cells each with its own nucleus. In a plant cell the rigid cellulose wall prevents cleavage. Two cells are formed by the secretion of a new cell wall in the region of the equatorial plate.

PROCESS OF MEIOSIS

Meiosis is another type of mitosis but requires two divisions for completion. Cytoplasmic events are similar in both divisions, but nuclear events are different. The first prophase is prolonged and usually divided into several substages. These stages and those of mitosis are purely artificial ones, used to make the study of both processes easier. Meiotic nuclei show a greater increase in volume and appear much larger than mitotic ones.

In meiosis, duplication of chromosomes occurs in the first prophase but probably in different stages of the prophase in various species of plants and animals.

In *leptotene,* or very early meiotic prophase, chromosomes appear as long single threads. There is not much coiling and the nucleolus is prominent. This is the stage of prophase when chromatin duplication often occurs, so that by the end of leptotene the chromatin threads may be double or bivalent.

In the *zygotene* stage, each like or *homologous* chromosome pairs up or *synapses* with the chromosome which is its mate and which controls the same characteristics. Shortly after the two homologous chromo-

somes synapse, each one of them splits. Each one of these double chromosomes lying side by side (synapsed) is called a *dyad*. Since the whole chromosome body is made up of four parts it is called a *tetrad*. The tetrads line up on the equatorial plate in metaphase.

Pachytene starts when pairing stops. It is one of the longer stages of meiotic prophase. Tetrad chromosomes shorten and thicken. Chromatids making up the bivalents are coiled around one another. The bivalents also coil around one another but in the opposite direction.

The next stage in meiotic prophase is called *diplotene*. Bivalents seem to repel one another. They pull away from each other except where they cross. Thus the chiasmata become very noticeable. As the paired chromosomes continue to condense, the chiasmata seem to slide off the ends of the chromosome pairs. Shortening seems to produce a kind of unravelling of the coils.

The final stage of the prophase is *diakinesis*. Tetrads migrate to the edge of the nucleus seeming to repel one another. Chiasmata are still prominent. The nucleolus becomes indistinct and disappears by the end of this stage. The nuclear membrane breaks up, releasing the tetrads into the cytoplasm.

Cytoplasmic events during this prophase are like those of mitosis so the spindle has already formed. Tetrads move to the equatorial plate and are oriented with centromeres toward the poles and arms toward the equatorial plate. Centromeres *do not* divide during this first metaphase.

In anaphase, bivalents, held together by their centromeres, migrate to the poles. Thus one bivalent chromosome from each pair enters a daughter cell. This reduces the total chromosome number by one half.

The second meiotic division is an ordinary mitotic one. In metaphase, the centromeres divide and the chromatids making up the bivalents separate and move to the poles.

Some species of plants and animals, like the spring flower Trillium and dragonflies, omit telophase, interphase, and the second prophase. Chromosomes wait in the cytoplasm until a new spindle forms. Thus, the second meiotic division begins with metaphase.

Genetic concepts, like crossover and random assortment of genes, are explained by the behavior of meiotic chromosomes.   J. C. K.
SEE ALSO: CELLS, HEREDITY, METABOLISM, REPRODUCTIVE SYSTEMS

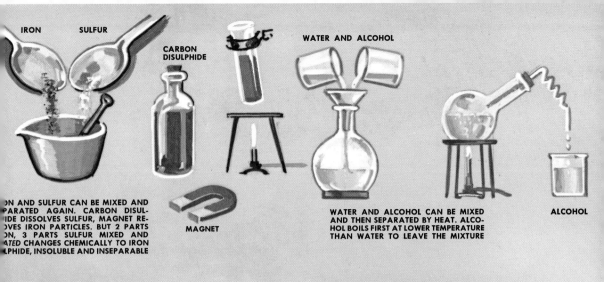

IRON SULFUR

CARBON DISULPHIDE

WATER AND ALCOHOL

)N AND SULFUR CAN BE MIXED AND
PARATED AGAIN. CARBON DISUL-
IDE DISSOLVES SULFUR, MAGNET RE-
OVES IRON PARTICLES. BUT 2 PARTS
)N, 3 PARTS SULFUR MIXED AND
ATED CHANGES CHEMICALLY TO IRON
LPHIDE, INSOLUBLE AND INSEPARABLE

MAGNET

WATER AND ALCOHOL CAN BE MIXED
AND THEN SEPARATED BY HEAT. ALCO-
HOL BOILS FIRST AT LOWER TEMPERATURE
THAN WATER TO LEAVE THE MIXTURE

ALCOHOL

Mixture A mixture is a substance made up of two or more elements or compounds mixed together. It is not like a chemical compound because no CHEMICAL CHANGE took place in the mixing. The parts of the mixture are not chemically united, and are present in any amount, not in some fixed proportion like a chemical compound.

Every component (part) of the mixture has the same properties or characteristics it had when it existed separately. It can be identified by these properties no matter how well it is mixed with something else. The mixture has no new properties of its own, as a compound does. For instance, iron filings and sulfur in a mixture do not change in appearance. They can be separated physically; that is, a magnet will draw out the filings, and carbon disulfide will dissolve the sulfur without affecting the iron. If the mixture is heated, however, a chemical change takes place, resulting in the new compound, iron sulfide. This differs from the mixture of iron and sulfur in that it has its own new set of properties and the components can not be separated physically.

There are many familiar mixtures. AIR is a mixture of elements; soil, SEA WATER, petroleum, and milk are mixtures of compounds.
E. R. B.
SEE ALSO: CHEMISTRY; COMPOUND; ELEMENTS; SUBSTANCES, PROPERTIES OF

Moa see Birds, flightless

Moccasin see Snakes

Moccasin flower see Wild flowers

Mock orange see Syringa

Mockingbird These birds are outstanding singers. They not only create a variety of musical phrases, but can borrow songs from other birds and interweave them with their own songs. This ability gives mockingbirds their name. Mockingbirds belong in the thrasher family, which is completely American. Most of them live in tropical South America; a few live in North America.

Mockingbirds are about the size of a robin, but slimmer. They are dark gray with gray-white bellies. The white patches on their wings and tail are distinctive in flight. The tails are long and wedge-shaped.

Mockingbird nests are built in thickets or low trees. They are made of twigs and weed stems, and lined with small roots, or cotton. Four to six green-blue eggs, spotted with brown, are laid. When the young leave, the parents raise another brood in a new nest.
J. C. K.

Moderator see Nuclear science glossary

Mockingbird

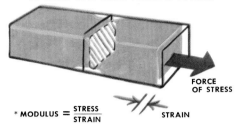

FORCE OF STRESS

* MODULUS = $\frac{STRESS}{STRAIN}$ STRAIN

The amount of stretching force or stress, divided by the stretch or strain that occurs in building materials produces a number, the modulus, that enables engineers to calculate the sizes of beams and girders needed in construction

Modulus (MAHJ-uh-luhs) Modulus is a number that represents to the engineer how much pulling or pushing FORCE a material will stand before it is in danger of weakening or breaking. Every day engineers design bridges and tall skyscrapers, automobiles and giant bulldozers, and many things of metal that must stand up under a great amount of stress and strain. To build strong and safe bridges, buildings and machines, the engineer must have a way of knowing in advance just how strong these structures will be if they are built in a certain way. One can imagine how dangerous and how wasteful it would be if a bridge were carelessly built. The modulus numbers give an engineer a way to figure out the right way to build things so that the structures will do the jobs they are supposed to do.

All materials are made of tiny particles called *molecules*. These molecules have large spaces between them, and in solid materials the molecules have great forces between them that cause the solids to resist any change in shape. The modulus numbers are obtained as the result of scientific experiments in laboratories. These numbers actually are measures of the strength of the attracting and repelling forces between the molecules of different materials.

The basic modulus of elasticity (or Young's modulus) gives a number value for each kind of material. The formula is:

Young's modulus = stress ÷ strain.

Stress is the stretching force (pounds) on the material per square inch of cross-sectional area; the strain is the inches of elongation per total inches of length. The modulus for each material is found experimentally.

SEE ALSO: ELASTICITY, MOLECULAR THEORY, MOLECULE, STRESS

Mohair see Goat

Mohave Desert see Desert

Moho Moho is a commonly used short term for *Mohorovicic Discontinuity*. Prof. A. Mohorovicic, a Yugoslavian geologist observed in 1909 that his instruments were recording shock waves of two distinct velocities from EARTHQUAKES deep inside the earth. From this he concluded that there must be two separate layers of rock quite different from each other far down below the surface.

It is now known that there are indeed two separate layers, one above the other. The upper layer of rock actually is the lowest layer of what is called the *earth's crust*. The lower of the two layers is the outer layer of the earth's mantle. The line which separates these two massive rock strata is called the *Mohorovicic Discontinuity*, or *Moho*.

Oceanographers using seismic sounding have further discovered that the Moho is from 3 to 8 miles (4.8 to 12.9 kilometers), and an average of 4 miles (6.4 kilometers), *below the sea*. By contrast it lies some 20 to 25 miles (32.2 to 40.2 kilometers) deep *under the continents*. This fact has destroyed the older notion that the earth's crust was relatively uniform in thickness. It is now shown that the crust is much thinner under

Moho is the line separating the earth's crust from the mantle

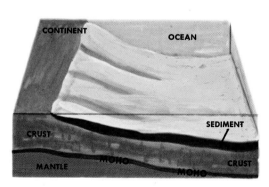

the oceans, and greatly thickened under the continents.

Above the Moho, the earth's crust under the oceans is made up first of a layer of sediment a few thousand feet thick. Below this is a thicker, heavier layer of sedimentary rock, sometimes called *Layer 2.* Below this is a layer of much denser basement rock, and under this is the Moho separating the crust from the mantle. On the CONTINENTS the basement rock sometimes appears on the surface as outcroppings, but it is consistently uniform under the oceans.   R.N.J.

SEE ALSO: ALTITUDE, DEPTH SOUNDING, EARTH, OCEANOGRAPHY, GEOLOGY

Moissan, Henri (1852-1907) Henri Moissan, a French inorganic chemist, was awarded the NOBEL PRIZE in chemistry in 1906.

Moissan's work had an important impact on industry. Moissan isolated *fluorine,* an important commercial element, in 1886. He developed the electric arc furnace. This he used in preparing and studying many important industrial compounds, such as calcium carbide. His production of artificial diamonds in 1893 was an outstanding achievement. His results, however, have not been reproducible, making chemists doubt the authenticity of the artificial diamond.   A.J.H.

Molar see Teeth

Molasses The thick, brownish-yellow syrup called molasses is made of sugar in water with small amounts of other plant-cell materials. It is used to cook, to make candy, to ferment into rum, and to feed farm animals.

Common molasses is a by-product of cane sugar making. The sap of cane is boiled with water until a thick, brown mass of liquid and crystals form. It is then whirled in a centrifuge-like drum with holes in its sides. The thinner liquid is thrown outward and collected as molasses, and the sugar crystals stay in the drum.

Molasses is about one-fourth water, two-thirds sugar, two and one-half per cent protein and three to six per cent cane-sap minerals.   D. A. B.

SEE ALSO: SUGARS

Mold Mold is the cottony, velvet-like, or powdery growth often found on old, rotting, and decayed food, plants, or animals. Mold grows in warm, moist places. It is a small fungus plant.

One mold plant is so tiny that it can be seen clearly only under a microscope. It takes many mold plants growing in one spot to show up on a piece of bread. Mold has thread-like structures which anchor it to its host. Little round heads form on the upright threads or branches. These heads are called *sporangium* or *spore cases.* Thousands of spores form in the spore cases. Mold does not contain CHLOROPHYLL, the material that is essential to the manufacture of food in plants. Mold cannot manufacture its own food, and so it is a parasitic or *saprophytic* growth that must get its food from other live or dead plants or animals, which are called *hosts.* When a spore from mold settles on a host, it bursts open and sends out hairlike threads. Spore cases develop on these threads. When they break open, air carries these spores to other areas where they develop into new plants. Soon the host is covered with mold.

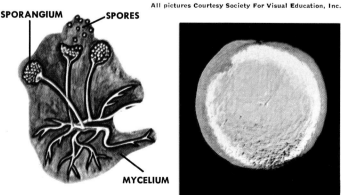

Slime mold seen closeup (left); diagram of parts of a mold plant (center); and penicillium mold on an orange (right)

All pictures Courtesy Society For Visual Education, Inc.

SPORANGIUM   SPORES

MYCELIUM

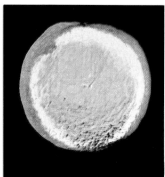

✳ **THINGS TO DO**

HOW TO GROW A MOLD GARDEN

1 **Expose a slice of bread to the air for an hour. Mold spores will fall upon it. Sprinkle the bread lightly with water and place in a covered glass jar. Put the jar in a warm, dark cupboard for a week. Bread mold has white stalks with little black balls on the ends. These are the spore cases.**
2 **Water mold can be made by placing several dead flies in a jar of water. In a few days the insects are covered with a white fuzz.**
3 **An orange, apple, or other fruit which has been bruised can be bottled. The mold and bacteria working on the fruit gradually caused it to disintegrate and rot. Penicillium molds are one type growing on fruits.**

Some molds are harmful and others are helpful to man. Black mold spoils bread and causes sweet potatoes and other crops to rot. Green mold grows on jelly and other kinds of food that are not properly cared for or refrigerated. Fruits affected with brown rot are said to be moldy. A gray mold can spread over some plants such as peonies, tulips, geraniums, and zinnias, and then they must be destroyed.

Molds are useful agents in decomposing waste materials and in making fertilizer. Molds enhance the flavor of such cheeses as Roquefort, Gorgonzola, and bleu.

Penicillin is a wonder drug derived from a soil mold. Its use in medicine brought about many advances in the treatment of infections.   M. R. L.

SEE ALSO: FUNGUS, PARASITE, PENICILLIN, SPORE FORMATION

Mole (mol) The mole is a fundamental unit in the INTERNATIONAL SYSTEM OF UNITS (SI). The mole is the SI unit for the amount of a substance. It is used mainly in chemistry.

The mole is defined as the amount of a substance of a system that contains as many elementary entities as there are atoms in .012 kilograms of carbon-12. In chemistry the mole is defined as the quantity of a species that contains Avogadro's number (6.02×10^{23}) of unit particles of the species.

The mole or gram-formula weight is the basis for quantitative chemistry. The mole is used in calculating mass-mass relationships in chemical equations, the number of atoms or molecules present, or the determination of empirical formulas.   A.J.H.

Mole (mammal) The work of the small but mighty mole can be seen on the ground. It leaves long ridges and "mole hills" as it tunnels in the earth. It has a stout body and stubby fur that feels like silk. Its eyes are tiny but this does not matter since it spends most of its life under the ground.

Moles belong to order INSECTIVORA, with their relatives the shrews. The *star-nosed mole* is unique. It has 22 tiny projections on its nose. Its fur is brownish-black and the front paws are paddle-like. It can be found in swamps and near streams in the middle states and north into Canada. It eats small water life as well as insects.

The *common* or *eastern mole* inhabits areas from the Atlantic coast to the Midwest. Its fur is copper to dark brown. It has five strong, digging claws. It nests below ground and has two to five babies.

The *western mole,* found along the Pacific coast, has brown fur. The smaller *hairy-tailed mole,* has a short, fat, hairy tail, while the tails of most moles are hairless.   H.J.C.

A mole

Molecular theory Scientists believe today that all matter is made up of small particles. When speaking of the physical behavior of matter, we usually call these particles MOLECULES, although they may, in many cases, be ATOMS or IONS. Whether a given piece of matter is SOLID, LIQUID, or GAS depends upon the spacing of its molecules and thus the pull of gravity between the molecules.

Today we have evidence for believing that, at any temperature above −273° C. (Absolute Zero) all molecules are in motion. We believe that it is this energy of molecular motion which is felt by our nerves as *heat*. When the molecules are vibrating strongly, and thus kept far apart, a sample of matter is in the gaseous state, as is air. But when we cool the sample of matter thus and slow down the molecules, they may "cuddle" closer together, and we have a *liquid*. In a liquid, the molecules are not as free to move as in a gas, although a liquid will readily flow and may be poured.

When the molecules are slowed down still more, by further cooling, they often line up in columns and rows alongside each other to form an orderly pattern called a *crystal* lattice. Our substance is now a solid with characteristic shape and rigidity.

Solutions are explained in this theory by assuming that there are spaces between the molecules of a liquid within which other, "foreign," molecules may fit. Because these foreign molecules disturb the normal intermolecular relations, solutions have a lower freezing temperature and a higher boiling temperature than is observed for a pure liquid alone.   C. F. R.
SEE ALSO: BROWNIAN MOVEMENT, COMPOUND, ELECTRON BORROWING, MOLECULE, NUCLEAR SCIENCE

Molecular weight For a particle as small as a MOLECULE, individual weights are not practical. Instead, a system of *relative weights,* based on atoms or molecules of certain elements, was chosen. Carbon (formerly oxygen = 16.000) is the standard.

Comparing a standard volume of hydrogen, the lightest element, with carbon (isotope C^{12}), shows that the same volume of carbon is 12.0000 times denser than hydrogen, if hydrogen is given the value 1.00797. Then the relative weights of all other elements are figured. Oxygen now has the value 15.9994, meaning an oxygen molecule is 15.9994/12.0000 times heavier than the standard carbon-12 particle.

The molecular weight of a compound such as water, H_2O, is thus the sum of the weights of all its atoms. The molecular weight of H_2O is $2 \times 1.00797 + 15.9994 = 18.01534$ units (= about 18.02). Since it is impossible to handle individual atoms, molecular (or formula) weight is often used in grams as *gram-molecular weight.* Water, thus, has a gram-molecular weight of about 18.02. This is also termed a *mole* of water. Chemists use the concept to calculate the products of combining chemicals:

$$2H_2 + 0_2 \qquad 2H_2O$$
$$(4.0319 \text{ gms}) + (31.9988 \text{ gms}) =$$
$$(36.0307 \text{ gms})$$

Two moles of hydrogen plus one mole of oxygen forms two moles of water.   D.A.B.
SEE ALSO: ATOM, CHEMISTRY, MOLECULAR THEORY

Molecules of H_2O in an ice crystal are bound together by forces between hydrogen atoms. The liquid state is produced when heat energy causes an increase in motion which overcomes the bond

Daniel Oldfield

Molecule (MAHL-uh-kue-uhl) All matter is made up of molecules. A molecule is the smallest particle that matter which is not a pure element can be broken down into and still have the physical and chemical properties of the original substance.

A *monatomic* element is one in which a molecule is composed of the same kind of atoms. The molecule of a *compound* is formed when different kinds of atoms combine. As examples, the formation of molecules from elements occurs when two atoms of hy-

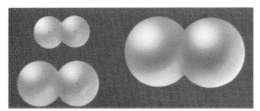

Diatomic molecules of gas are two atoms of the particular element

drogen, oxygen, chlorine, or nitrogen combine. These gases are considered diatomic and their chemical formulas, which are H_2, O_2, N_2, indicate that. Those that have more than two atoms are called *polyatomic* molecules.

The molecule of a compound is formed when different kinds of atoms combine.

The atoms in a molecule take the position of *minimum potential energy*. If pushed together or pulled apart, they will spring back to the original position. These different positions depend on the temperature, pressure, and other conditions to which these molecules are subjected.

The molecules of various substances do not change in composition because of a physical change of the SUBSTANCE. The substance may be in any of the three states (LIQUID, SOLID, GAS), but the molecules will be made up of the same atoms. The difference in the molecules, depending on the state, is the distance the molecules are from each other. Molecules in the gaseous state are relatively far apart. These molecules are moving with high velocities, bumping each other or the walls of their container. This constant push against the container creates what is called *gas pressure*.

Molecules in the liquid state have less energy than in a gas, and they make and break connections while moving about. The movement of molecules in a liquid and gas is shown by the BROWNIAN MOVEMENT. In a solid state the molecules are confined to definite spaces where least movement occurs. According to the kinetic molecular theory, molecules are moving constantly whenever they are at temperatures above $-273°$ C (absolute zero); they would come to a standstill if absolute zero were reached. E. Y. K.

SEE ALSO: KINETIC THEORY, MATTER, MOLECULAR THEORY, MOLECULAR WEIGHT

Mollusca (mul-LUSS-kuh) The word *molluscus* means soft. People who have eaten oysters and clams know that these animals have soft, fleshy bodies. Mollusca is the name for one of the large groups of animals without backbones, those animals that are called *invertebrates*.

Most mollusks, like the CUTTLEFISH, WHELK, and OCTOPUS, live in the ocean. However, some, like the SNAILS, are also found in fresh water and on land. Most mollusks have hard shells. Some shells have beautiful colors. Many mollusks are quite large. One giant clam weighs 1000 pounds (453.59 kilograms); the SQUID may grow to 50 feet (15.24 meters).

Mollusks have compact bodies. The entire bottom surface forms a fleshy foot. Above this lies a jelly-like mass, consisting of the body organs. Since most mollusks carry their organs on their backs, they appear to be "top-heavy." Covering these delicate organs is a body wall, called a *mantle*. When a shell is present, it is produced by the cells of the mantle. Between the organs and the mantle, there is a space called the *mantle cavity*. Rows of GILLS are usually found in this cavity. In land mollusks, the gills are replaced by a type of lung.

Mollusks have a unique tool for cutting food. A tongue-like organ, called a *radula*, may be extended from the mouth cavity. This is covered with rows of tiny teeth. As it is slid back and forth, like a cross-cut saw, it shaves off tiny pieces of food. One large whelk uses the radula to bore through clam and oyster shells.

These animals have been divided into five main classes. The most primitive group is made up mainly of the CHITONS, or *sea cradles*. These creatures wear a shell made of eight overlapping plates. This allows for such flexibility that the chiton can curl up like a ball and rock like a cradle. The curling up gives it protection.

The *scaphopods, or* "tooth-shells," can be mistaken for elephant's tusks. The shell is a single long tube, open at both ends. When the foot, which protrudes from one end, is

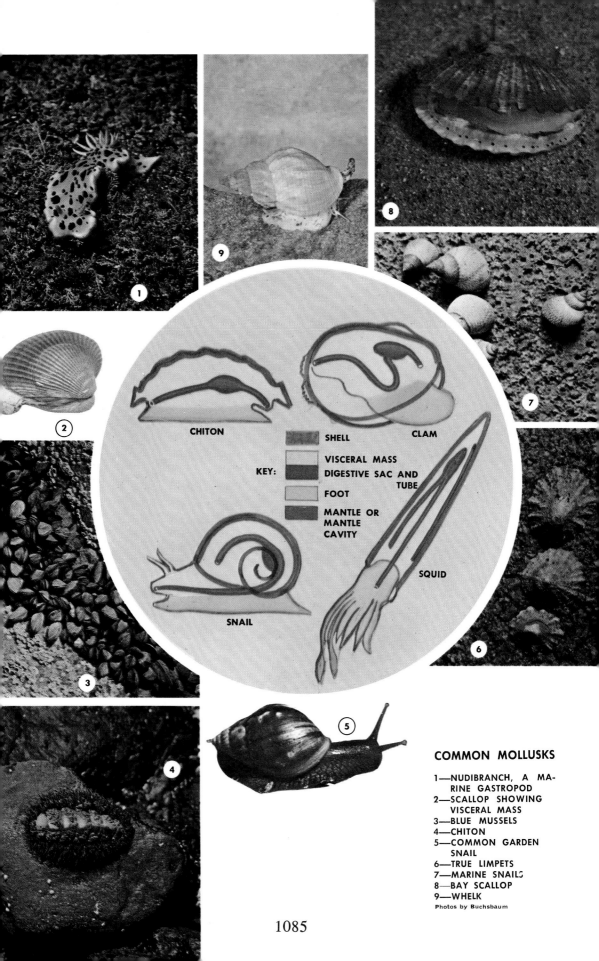

KEY:
- SHELL
- VISCERAL MASS
- DIGESTIVE SAC AND TUBE
- FOOT
- MANTLE OR MANTLE CAVITY

CHITON

CLAM

SNAIL

SQUID

COMMON MOLLUSKS

1—NUDIBRANCH, A MA-
RINE GASTROPOD
2—SCALLOP SHOWING
VISCERAL MASS
3—BLUE MUSSELS
4—CHITON
5—COMMON GARDEN
SNAIL
6—TRUE LIMPETS
7—MARINE SNAILS
8—BAY SCALLOP
9—WHELK

Photos by Buchsbaum

1085

✳ THINGS TO DO

OBSERVING MARINE LIFE

1 inch =
2.5 centimeters

A salt-water aquarium will serve as a satisfactory home for live mollusks or shellfish. The tank should have a wide open top to permit a large surface of water to be exposed to oxygen in the air.

1 Put two inches of clean sand on the bottom of the tank. Make sea water by following this recipe: 4 quarts of water, 3 ounces of salt (sodium chloride), a few grains each of potassium sulfate, magnesium chloride, and magnesium sulfate. Pour a few inches of this sea water over the sand.

2 Root live seaweed, water grass, and Irish moss in the sand. Place a paper over the water and plants while you finish filling the tank. The paper spreads the water to prevent stirring up the sand.

3 Now the ocean home is ready for inhabitants. If you live along the seashore, mollusks may be captured first hand. Inland one must purchase them from a supply house. Interesting animals to raise are baby octopi, squids, mussels, snails, limpets, or scallops. Be sure to determine which animals can live together.

buried in the sandy sea bottom, the stiff shell slants upward, like a stick.

The *gastropods,* or "stomach-footed" mollusks, have a one-piece shell which they carry on their backs. However, some gastropods do not have an outside shell. The SLUG, for example, has a thin shell buried in the mantle. Snails and whelks have beautiful, coiled shells, into which most are able to withdraw for protection. These animals usually have well-developed heads with eyes and tentacles.

CLAMS, OYSTERS, and MUSSELS are *pelecypods* or "hatchet-footed" mollusks. This name is derived from the shape of the fleshy foot which is used as a burrowing tool to pull the animal through the sand. Since the shell is made of two pieces hinged together, pelecypods are also called *bivalves,* meaning "two doors." Pelecypods are sluggish animals, without heads. Since the shell is so heavy, they often remain buried in the sand or attached by one shell to a rock, while the other shell acts as a lid. These animals have no radula. Microscopic organisms are strained from the water which enters the mantle cavity through a tube or siphon.

The most highly-developed mollusks are the *cephalopods,* meaning "head-footed." They have a foot divided into a number of arms, which circle the head. While the NAUTILUS has an exquisitely coiled, pearly shell, the squid has only a shell plate buried in the mantle, while the octopus has no shell.

Cephalopods are quite powerful animals; they prey upon larger animals of the sea. The arms are used both for crawling and for capturing food. The tentacles are equipped with suckers, within which are often found sharp, chitinous teeth. The squid and the octopus are also able to move by jet propulsion. Water is taken under the mantle and pushed out with great force through a siphon.

Until 1952, mollusks were thought to be unsegmented. At that time ten living specimens of a mollusk (Neopalina), formerly known only as a fossil, were dredged from the sea. These showed segmented muscles, nephridia, and gills. This may show that ANNELIDA and mollusks are more closely related than was thought.

In the mollusk's *visceral mass* are well-formed digestive, nervous, reproductive, and circulatory systems. Squids and octopi have camera eyes similar to those of man. E. P. L.
SEE ALSO: ANIMALS, CLASSIFICATION OF

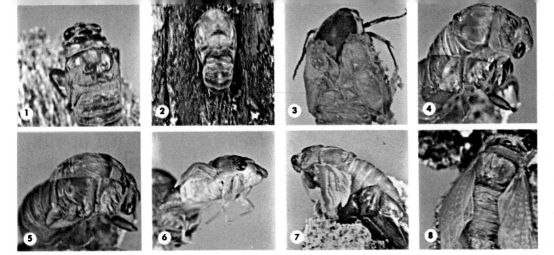

The seventeen-year cicada emerges from the ground as a nymph (1). As part of its metamorphosis, it climbs a tree and sheds its skin, starting with a split at the thorax (2, 3). The feet are pulled out (4) and the head and thorax emerge (5). The abdomen comes into view last (6). The adult emerges with the wings moist and crumpled (7). They then hang downward to unfold and dry (8)

Molting Molting is the shedding of its outer covering by an animal. Crayfish and insects shed their outer skeletons; birds, their feathers; snakes, their skins; and man, his hair.

Young birds have four types of plumage during their first year. They molt to acquire each kind. They begin with *down,* then acquire *juvenal* feathers, *winter plumage,* and *nuptial,* or spring plumage. Thereafter, birds alternate between winter and spring plumages. Birds like eagles, who need three to five years to mature, have several winter and spring plumages before acquiring adult dress. Molting is probably controlled by both GONAD and PITUITARY HORMONES.

Skin shedding by amphibians and reptiles and loss of hair by MAMMALS is also thought to be under hormonal control. Different hormones or hormone combinations may be involved in different animals. For example, in the *varying hare,* shedding of a white winter coat and replacement by a brown is controlled by *pituitary gonadotropins* (pituitary hormones controlling a gonad). In frogs, molting is associated with METAMORPHOSIS. In preparation for a molt, the outer skin thickens by cell division. This is controlled by pituitary and ADRENAL hormones. Shedding is controlled by the THYROID gland.

Among ARTHROPODA, *neurosecretory* cells produce hormones which control molting. Glands making the hormone are called

A molting snake

neurohemal organs. In crustacea, molting involves withdrawal and storage of calcium, a rapid intake of water to split the shell, and secretion of a new shell. *X organs* in the eyestalk ganglia produce a hormone that is stored in eyestalk *sinus glands.* It acts on *Y organs,* in the first or antennary segment, to inhibit the production of *ecdysone,* the molting hormone. Molting thus depends upon the concentration of the X-organ hormone. When low, a molt occurs.   J. C. K.

SEE ALSO: ARTHRODPODA, INSECTA, MAMMALIA, METAMORPHOSIS

Molybdenum   (muh-LIBB-duh-num) The element molybdenum was first isolated in 1782 by P. J. Hjelm. Molybdenum (chemical symbol Mo) is element number 42. It is a metal similar to iron.

Molybdenum ALLOY steel is very strong. Mo is added in small amounts with other metals to produce a strong, tough steel that resists strains without breaking. These alloys are used for making automobile parts.

Molybdenum is purified from *molybdenite* ore. The ore looks very much like lead and the element was named for the Greek word for lead. Molybdenum has an atomic weight of 95.94.   J. R. S.

SEE ALSO: ATOM, ELEMENTS

Moment In mechanics, moment is the tendency, or the measure of the tendency, to cause rotation, especially about an axis. It is the product of the force and its perpendicular distance from the axis.

THINGS TO DO

DEMONSTRATING MOMENTUM

1. Place two nickels, a dime, and a quarter equal distances apart on a smooth surface. With a ruler, push the quarter so that it slides into one nickel. Push the dime with the same speed into the other nickel.
2. The first nickel moved farther than the other because a quarter has more mass than a dime. It would give more motion than the dime would.
3. Mark the resting positions of the two nickels. Slide one into the other.
4. Note that the nickel that was hit did not move as far as the one that was pushed. While they have the same mass, the energy lost by the hit coin was given up in friction.   **A. E. L.**

Momentum (moh-MENN-tum) Momentum is the quantity of MOTION of a moving mass. A large mass with a certain velocity has a greater momentum than does a small MASS with the same velocity. Equal masses moving with equal velocities possess the same quantity of motion. If equal masses have different velocities, then the mass having the greater velocity has the greater momentum. Hence, momentum depends on both the mass of the body and the VELOCITY with which the body is moving. It is measured by the product of the mass and the velocity or: $M = mv$. M equals the momentum, m is the mass of the body, and v is its velocity.

Since momentum is a *vector* quantity, it must have both magnitude and direction. To change these properties, a body possessing

momentum must be acted upon by some "extra" or external force. The action of an external force on a body is called *impulse*. Impulse depends on the amount of time the force is allowed to act on the system. If the force is constant in magnitude, impulse is shown by the formula: $IMP = Ft$, where t is the total time the force F acts on the body.

From the above, it is evident that a system which is free from the actions of external forces, called an *isolated system,* must maintain a constant level of momentum. Not evident, but still true, is the fact that the direction of the momentum must also remain constant. These facts lead to an extremely important property called the *principle of the conservation of momentum.* This principle, in general, is: *the total momentum of an isolated system is constant in both magnitude and direction.* To obtain an isolated system for the purpose of demonstrating this principle in an elementary fashion is practically impossible. All mechanical systems used to demonstrate this principle are subject to frictional forces, which are external forces.

The conservation of momentum becomes increasingly important where bodies are not acted upon by any external force such as friction. In the investigation of the energies transferred when subatomic particles collide, the principles of the conservation of momentum are indispensable.   **A. E. L.**
SEE ALSO: ELASTICITY, FORCE, INERTIA

Monarch see Butterflies

Monel metal Monel metal is a silvery white ALLOY of about two-thirds NICKEL and one-third COPPER, with small quantities of other metals. It is resistant to corrosion, has a bright finish, and is as hard as STEEL, yet it is easy to forge and prepare.

Monera Monera is a kingdom of living things. Blue-green algae and bacteria are classified in this group. They show little organization, yet they carry on all life processes. They have no membrane around the nucleus. They lack organized plastids and mitochondria.

Mongolism Mongolism (also called Down's syndrome) is one type of birth defect. Children with this defect have close-set, slanting eyes, a broad, flat skull, and a large, thick tongue. The inherited defect is an extra number 21 CHROMOSOME.

Mongoloid see Evolution of man

Mongoose

Mongoose (MAHNG-goos) This is a small animal in the skunk-weasel family. There are about 40 species of mongooses living in the warmer parts of the world such as Malay, India, and Africa. They are good fighters killing birds, small mammals, and poisonous snakes. Most of them are fond of eggs.

Mongooses have long bodies, bushy tails, and rounded ears. Their fur is brownish and their legs short. The feet have five toes and claws that are not retractable.

The mongooses are the top CARNIVORES of the community. They occupy the niche or place that weasels occupy in their range. Mongooses have been imported to various places to control rat and snake populations. However, they have bred rapidly and have become pests. They have two to four young every year. J. C. K.
SEE ALSO: CARNIVORE

Monkey The monkey belongs to the most highly developed order of mammals, the PRIMATES. Other primates are lemurs, man-like apes, and man. The monkey usually has a tail and a short, narrow, man-like face. Monkeys live in tropical jungles near rivers and streams, feeding on insects, fruit, and plants at sunrise and sunset. Some eat the flesh of small animals. All can use their feet as hands and their arms are usually longer than their legs.

Most monkeys have an *opposable* great toe which serves them in the same manner as the thumbs on their hands. They are able to grasp objects with both feet and hands. Monkey's eyes are directed downward. They have binocular vision which is very similar to that in man.

There are two large groups of monkeys. The *Old World* monkey lives in Africa and Asia. The only monkeys in Europe are the *Barbary apes*. These are not true apes, resembling apes only in the absence of a tail. These have been protected by the British government since the early eighteenth century because, according to tradition, as long as these monkeys live upon the Rock of Gibraltar, the British will be able to keep possession of that rock.

The Old World monkeys have nostrils which open downward and 32 teeth. They have pouches and thick-skinned buttocks, and some have brilliant, colored markings. Many of them are tailless and if they have a tail it is not used in climbing. The rhesus monkey, in which the "RH FACTOR" was discovered, is an Old World monkey.

The *New World monkeys* inhabit the tropics of South America, and the southern part of Mexico. The nose is flat and the nostrils are widely separated and open on the side. Most of them have tails called *prehensile* tails, which they use in tree-top travel. They are without pouch or thick skin on the buttocks. They have four more teeth than the Old World monkey. The best known variety is the light-colored *capuchin* monkey with a hood-shaped shock of hair on its head. G. A. D.
SEE ALSO: MAMMALIA

New world monkeys have prehensile tails that help them travel through trees.

Christine Hagel

Courtesy Society For Visual Education, Inc.

Indian cucumber-root (above) shows the linear-veined leaves of a monocot. Monocot seeds are encased in a fruit (right)

Monocotyledon A monocotyledon is a flowering plant with only one embryo seed leaf (cotyledon).

Over 40,000 species of flowering plants are monocotyledons. They include bamboo, corn, palms, bananas, pineapples, onions, lilies, irises, orchids, wheat, barley and other grasses, as well as some water plants—arrowhead, waterweed, eelgrass, pondweed, surf grass, and tape grass. The LEAVES of these plants usually have linear veins and smooth edges. Their stems are slender and often have prominent joints or nodes. The fluid-conducting tubes (*fibrovascular bundles*) are scattered throughout the stem tissue. The parts of monocotyledon flowers (sepals, petals, stamens, carpels) are found in multiples of three. D. J. A.

SEE ALSO: COTYLEDON, DICOTYLEDON

Monoecious (moan-EE-shuss) Monoecious refers to a plant whose flowers each have only a STAMEN or a PISTIL, not both. Both kinds of flowers—staminate and pistillate — however, are borne on the same plant. Oak trees and corn are examples. The term is also applied to hermaphroditic animals (those with both male and female sex organs in the same individual).

SEE: DIOECIOUS, HERMAPHRODITE

Mononucleosis (MAHN-uh-new-klee-OH-sis) Mononucleosis, or infectious mononucleosis, is an acute disease lasting from one to three weeks. It may linger for one to three months. Formerly it was called *glandular fever,* and that term accurately describes the main features of a typical attack. The first symptoms are fever, weakness, headache, and chills. Then it is noticed that the glands of the neck are swollen, sometimes, but not necessarily, following a sore throat.

Mononucleosis is caused by a VIRUS called the Epstein-Barr virus, which in other countries also causes lymph, nose, and throat tumors. It is transmitted by saliva (in a third of patients) and occasionally via blood transfusion. Most people have antibodies to the virus without ever having been very ill.

Patients usually get well without complication. Occasionally, more severe symptoms develop, such as chest pains, coughing, and difficulty in breathing. Even JAUNDICE has been noticed in some cases, but the chief discomfort comes from the fever, swollen glands, and irritation inside the throat.

In addition to identifying the triad of symptoms found in typical cases, two other measures are necessary. A blood smear must be made. In mononucleosis a great increase of *lymphocytes* is found. The *leucocyte* (white blood cell) level may increase.

The great number of lymphocytes causes changes in the LIVER and the SPLEEN. The liver becomes infiltrated with lymphocytes and may simulate hepatitis. Even a positive infectious HEPATITIS may present typical lymphocytes in the blood, and the two diseases can only be differentiated on occasion by an agglutination blood test.

The treatment is directed for the most part at allaying the troublesome symptoms, such as the sore throat and the high fever. ANTIBIOTICS are useless, and STEROIDS are of questionable value. Bed rest at the time of fever and spleen enlargement is important, and should probably be maintained if jaundice or other complications are present.

H.K.S./E.S.S.

SEE ALSO: BLOOD, LYMPHATIC SYSTEM

A monorail of the future

Monorail A monorail is a type of machine, such as a carriage or truck, which moves on a single rail or cable. Experiments have been conducted on trains suspended beneath a monorail and running on pneumatic tires, and trains running on a monorail balanced by a gyroscope.

SEE: MACHINERY; TRAIN, RAILROAD

Monotreme A monotreme is an animal belonging to the most primitive order of mammals—*Monotremata.* The DUCKBILL, or *platypus,* and SPINY ANTEATER *(Echidna)* are the only members of the order. They both lay eggs and nurse their young.

SEE: MAMMALIA

Monsoon (mahn-SOON) A monsoon is, in the general sense of the term, a wind that blows in one direction for many months, up to half a year. According to a special meaning, a monsoon refers to the southerly ocean winds that bring to India the summer season of heavy rains. Monsoon winds, by either meaning, affect tropical weather much as spring thaws and first seasonal snowfalls signal changes to people of temperate lands. Such seasonal winds occur not only in Asia but also in Africa and parts of tropical America.

In India, the dry season comes in the winter months. Then dry cold winds blow from Sibera over India toward the Indian Ocean. As air becomes warmer, it can hold more WATER VAPOR. Since the winter winds are blowing toward warmer regions, no rain occurs. After the winter winds die down, winds begin to blow from the Indian Ocean. over India. The moisture-laden air over the ocean is cooler than the intensely-heated air over the land. The cooler air is more dense and exerts more pressure than the less dense air over the land. As the air moves over the land, it is elevated and cooled and releases its moisture as rain. In India the rainy season usually lasts from June until September or October.

In winter, India lies in the northeast trade wind belt. These winds blow steadily from the northeast toward the equator. In summer, the southeast trade winds prevail. The southeast trade winds (normally below the equator) shift northward in summer. Both these winds blow steadily for many months to produce the prolonged wet and dry seasons.   P. F. D.

SEE ALSO: ASIA, CLIMATE

Month see Calendar, Earth, Moon

A northeast monsoon during the winter

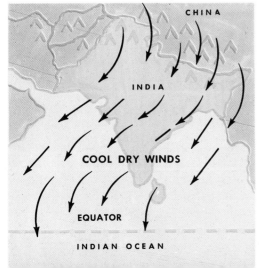

COOL DRY WINDS

EQUATOR

INDIAN OCEAN

CHINA

INDIA

A southwest monsoon during the summer

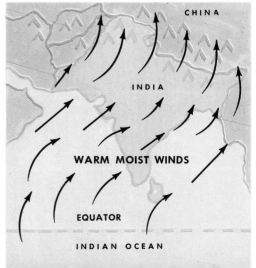

WARM MOIST WINDS

EQUATOR

INDIAN OCEAN

CHINA

INDIA

Moon The moon is the Earth's natural satellite. It revolves around the Earth in a little less than 30 days. The Earth is four times as large as the moon. The word *lunar* refers to the moon.

One can see the moon when sun's light is reflected off the surface. The side of the moon facing the sun is very hot, while the side away from the sun is very cold. There are great temperature extremes between these two sides and scientists believe unprotected life could not exist there.

The moon is the only natural SATELLITE (small body associated with a large one) of the Earth. Some other planets have more satellites, but in proportion to its size, Earth has the largest satellite. The moon has a diameter of 2,160 miles (3,480 kilometers). It is the closest heavenly body to the Earth. Its average distance from Earth is 238,000 miles (383,000 kilometers). Because it is so near, to people on Earth the moon looks nearly as large as the sun.

The moon's surface has mountains, craters, and large flat areas called seas on it.

NASA

This surface, which looks crystal-like, is actually covered with a clinging black dust.

The moon has three kinds of motion. It *revolves* around the earth. It *rotates* on its axis. It *follows* the earth in a journey around the sun. The moon always keeps the same side facing the earth. Therefore, its period of rotation is the same as its period of revolution around the earth—about 28 days. Its average speed in its orbit is 0.63 miles (1 kilometer) per second.

Since the moon always shows the same side to the earth, men cannot see the other side of the moon. On October 6, 1959, *Lunik III,* a Russian moon probe, sent televised pictures of the other side of the moon to Earth.

Even with the naked eye, one can see the shadings of the moon. People have often thought they resembled a face, which is the reason for the expression "the man in the moon." Shady areas on the moon are caused by the differences in the composition of various areas of the moon's surface. Some substances are better reflectors of light than others. When the moon is in a phase that gives a partial view of the half than can be seen, irregularities along the inside edge of the moon are visible. These are caused by the differences in the level of the ground there.

With the use of modern TELESCOPES, much detail of the moon's surface may be seen. The moon surface is made up of mountains, craters, and large flat areas called "seas." There appear to be two types of mountains on the moon. There are a few that seem to be similar to some of the mountains found on Earth, but most are of the type that occur

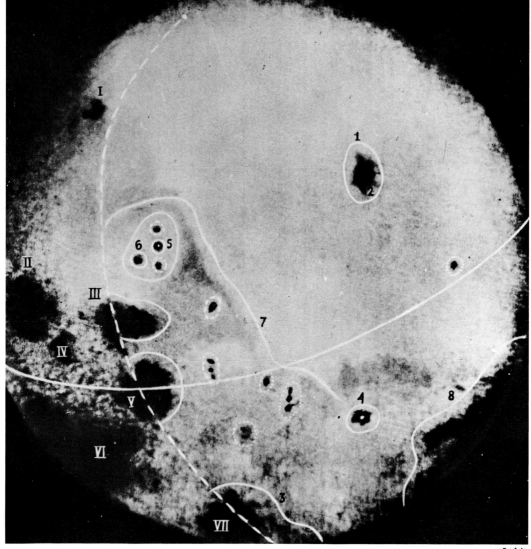

Physical features of the back side of the moon were first seen in photos taken by a Russian lunar probe satellite. A composite chart shows the equator at the continuous line and the division between the visible and invisible hemispheres at the broken lines. Features circled with a continuous line have been definitely established. The others require further study. Features labeled 1, 2, 3, and 8 are maria, or "seas;" for example, the Sea of Dreams at 8. 4, 5, and 6 are craters. 7 is a mountain range. Roman numerals I through VII are on the visible part of the moon and are known to be maria

as circular ridges in association with the craters. The lunar seas are somewhat like the plains of Earth but are dotted by large and small craters. Lunar seas do not contain any water. There is evidence that these seas were probably formed by slow but extensive lava flows. Soft landing of space vehicles has shown the surface of the moon to be much like that of the Earth.

The craters on the moon are the most noticeable surface markings. The moon seems to be nearly covered with these circular, sunken formations which are surrounded by sharp, jagged ridges. Whitish streaks or rays radiate from some of the craters. What has caused the lunar craters is another question that has not been definitely answered.

Some astronomers believe that they were made many years ago by volcanic eruptions on the moon. There may have been a hot fluid or lava inside the moon that caused swelling and broke through the crust of the moon's surface. A collapse of the central area could have created the craters as seen today. Other astronomers believe that the craters were formed by the collisions of METEORS with the moon. The sunken lunar craters could easily have been formed by the explosions of meteors.

In spite of the names given to the maria of the moon (for instance the Sea of Serenity, the Sea of Tranquillity, the Lake of Sleep) astronomers are not able to detect the existence of water on the moon.

Moon, phases of

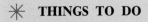

✳ THINGS TO DO

WHAT IS THE POSITION OF A NEW MOON IN THE SKY?

Materials: a lamp without a shade, and a light-colored ball

1 In a darkened room, hold the ball out in front of you so it is in line with your eyes and the bulb in the lamp. The light is the sun, the ball the moon, and you are on the earth.

2 Now move the moon slightly to the left of the bulb. How much of the moon is lighted at this point? This is a new moon.

3 Keep rotating with the ball in front of you. At which point is there a full moon?

If there were water there, astronomers would be able to notice effects such as EROSION of rocks, drainage from high to low places, and valleys in the mountain ranges. None of these effects can be seen. It is possible that long ago there was a little water on the moon.

The gravitational force on the moon is much less than that on Earth. The low GRAVITY of the moon has been unable to hold onto much ATMOSPHERE. Most astronomers believe that there is no atmosphere on the moon. Others say that there may be a very little. But whatever atmosphere the moon might have would probably be less than that of the best VACUUM men can make on Earth. The ASTRONAUTS who visit the moon need to take their own supply of oxygen along.

Without atmosphere, sound cannot travel. Communication on the moon has to be by wireless or by radiotelephone.

Because there is no atmosphere on the moon, areas in shade are completely dark and cold. In direct sunlight the temperature reaches as high as 212° F. (100° C.). In an unlighted place the temperature goes down to −238° F. (−149° C.).

The purpose of the National Aeronautics and Space Administration Apollo Program was to place a man on the moon. The Apollo Program was preceded by the Surveyor Program that made both hard and soft landings on the moon. The early Apollo flights orbited the moon photographing possible landing sites. These flights paved the way for the historic Apollo 11 flight. On July 21, 1969, astronaut Neil A. Armstrong became the first man to step on the moon. A few minutes later he was joined by Edwin E. Aldrin, Jr. The men spent over two hours on the moon setting up equipment and gathering samples on the moon's surface.

In all, five more Apollo flights landed on the moon. The astronauts performed various experiments and brought back many rocks from the moon. One rock, called the Genesis rock, is estimated to be 4.15 billion years old. Other rocks brought back on Apollo 17, the last moon flight, were orange and red, indicating possible volcanism on the moon.　　　H.S.G.

SEE ALSO: EARTH, ECLIPSE, LUNAR BASE, SOLAR SYSTEM, SUN, TIDES

Moon, phases of From Earth the moon's shape seems to change from night to night. The different shapes of the lighted part of the moon that can be seen from earth are called *phases*. The moon's real shape is almost like a ball. Sometimes it is seen as a full bright disk, sometimes as half a disk. Sometimes there is only a small silver crescent. Sometimes no moon can be seen at all. The changes of the moon's shape are caused by its different positions as it revolves around the earth.

One half of the moon's globe is lighted by the SUN. One half of the moon can be seen from Earth. Man sees only the fully lighted half of the moon when Earth is between the moon and the sun. When the moon is between Earth and the sun, the lighted half is turned completely away from the earth. Then the moon cannot be seen. During the time that the moon is between these two positions, only portions of the lighted half of the moon are seen.

The moon makes a complete journey around the earth in about 28 days. During this time the moon goes through all of its phases. When all of the lighted half of the moon is seen, the phase is called *full moon*. When no moon appears, the phase is *new moon*. When there is only a slim sliver of the moon, the phase is *crescent*. When one-half of the lighted half of the moon is seen, the phase is called *quarter moon*. As the moon goes from quarter position to full moon position, the straight side of the moon begins to bulge. It looks like a lop-sided ball. This phase is the *gibbous* moon.

As the moon goes from new moon to full moon, its shape grows larger. This is called its *waxing* period. As it goes from full back to new moon again, it is said to be *waning*. During the waning period the moon's shape gets smaller. When the moon is waxing the right portions of the moon appear lighted. When the moon is waning, the light is on the left portions. Waxing phases face left. Waning phases face right. The waxing quarter phase is called *first quarter*. The waning quarter phase is the *third quarter*.

Sometimes at new moon, when the moon is between the earth and the sun, the moon's outline is only faintly lighted. This is sometimes called "the new moon in the old moon's arms."　　　　　C. L. K.
SEE ALSO: MOON; SATELLITE, NATURAL; SOLAR SYSTEM

Moonflower see Morning-glory

Moonstone see Feldspar

Moor A moor is open land, either flat and plain-like, or rolling and rugged with ravines and cuts.

Moors are found in various parts of the North American continent and Europe. When speaking of moors, however, one usually thinks of the British Isles where peat-covered moorlands are common.　　D. J. I.

Moose see Deer family

Moraine (moh-RAIN) A moraine is a mass of stones and earth deposited by melting glacial ice. Many of the large boulders and earth formations in the northern United States remain from the melting GLACIERS of the Glacial Ice Age.

Moraines are classified according to the pattern in which rocks and earth were left by a glacier. Major types of moraines are the terminal, lateral, medial, and ground.

Glaciers do not sort the material they carry; the material is of all sizes. The moraine left at the end of the glacier after it melts is called a *terminal moraine*. It is usually piled up in an irregular ridge, or hill, and marks the farthest point the glacier reached. The unsorted material in a moraine is often called *glacial drift* or *till*.

Lateral moraines consist of earth and rocks heaped along the margins of a glacier. Lateral moraines leave two somewhat parallel lines of material by which the path of a glacier may be traced.

Medial moraines occur where two valley glaciers came together. The lateral moraines of each join to form a medial (middle) moraine down the center of the new larger glacier, forming the shape of a large Y.

A *ground* moraine consists of earth and rock that are deposited beneath a melting glacier.　　　　　P. F. D.
SEE ALSO: GEOLOGY, GLACIAL AGES

Moray see Eel

The ridge of broken rock is a lateral moraine

Mordant A mordant is a substance or combination of substances used to produce a deeper color in dyeing or to make a dye remain permanently in a fiber. Salts of metals, acids or hydroxides are used depending on the dye and fabric used.

SEE: DYES

Morel

Morel This plant cannot make its own food. It lacks the green coloring, chlorophyll. Morels belong in the group of simple plants called FUNGI. They grow on, and get their food from, dead vegetation.

Structurally, morels are made of two parts. The fruiting body is a yellowish-brown cap which is spongelike. It grows upon a white upright stalk. Reproduction is by means of spores, produced in cavities on the outside of the fruiting body and dispersed by wind.

Morels are sac fungi in the class Ascomycetes.   H. J. C.

SEE ALSO: FUNGUS

Morning glory The morning glory plant may be a clinging vine or a low bush. The flowers which appear in the late summer come in many colors, but blue is the most common. The blossom is in the shape of a cone or trumpet. It is an annual so seeds must be planted each year.

The herbaceous stem of this climber may reach up 12 feet (3.66 meters) high if it has a trellis or support. It grows around the support in a touch response called *thigmotropism.*

The leaves are alternate with wavy edges. The flower may be 4 inches (10.16 centimeters) wide, though one variety has been grown with 8-inch (20.32-centimeter) blooms. The plant should not be permitted

Morning-glory blossoms open with the sun and close in later afternoon
Courtesy Society For Visual Education, Inc.

to sow itself, as inferior plants develop. Seeds should be planted in an area that gets full sunshine and in ordinary humus.

There is a family of plants called the morning-glory family. It includes the sweet potato, dodder, and other parasitic species which attack some grasses.   H.J.C.

Morphine (MAWR-feen) Morphine is a drug used in medicine. It is used to relieve pain and sometimes to bring on a deep sleep. It was named after Morpheus, the Greek god of dreams. Morphine and its derivative *heroin* are habit-forming drugs, narcotics. Morphine comes from a plant, the *opium poppy.*

Morphine is the main active ingredient of OPIUM. The pharmacist makes it into a powder for medicinal purposes. It cannot be purchased without a prescription written by a doctor. In medicine, morphine is always used in the form of one of its salts, usually the *hydrochloride.* Its use must be regulated carefully by the doctor. An overdose of morphine can cause a stupor, coma, or even death. When morphine is taken too often, it becomes a habit. It becomes necessary to have more and more, because the lack of it causes the addict to be sick and suffer great pain. Morphine has been used for over a thousand years.   M. R. L.

SEE ALSO: NARCOTICS, PHARMACOLOGY

Morphology (more-FAHL-uh-gee) Morphology is that branch of BIOLOGY which deals with the form and structure of plants and animals. Because structural differences in different species are so obvious, morphology has always been important in the classification of plant and animal life.

SEE: ANATOMY; ANIMALS, CLASSIFICATION OF; PLANTS, CLASSIFICATION OF

Samuel Morse invented the telegraph and Morse code

Morse, Samuel Finley Breese (1791-1872) Samuel Morse was the American who invented the most widely used telegraph. He also developed the Morse code, an alphabet consisting of dots and dashes to be used in sending messages.

In addition to his inventive genius, Morse was one of the finest American artists of his day, being especially gifted in portrait painting. He was the founder of the National Academy of Design in New York City and served for nineteen years as its first president.

The son of a well-known and highly respected clergyman and geographer, Morse was born at Charlestown, Massachusetts. He received his education at Yale College, but he was not a serious student. He developed a fervent interest in painting miniature portraits and wanted to study art in London.

In 1832 Samuel Morse returned to Europe, intending to study art, but on his trip across he became engaged in a dinner conversation that changed his entire life.

Through it he conceived the idea of building a single-circuit electromagnetic TELEGRAPH. Although electric telegraphs had been proposed, and JOSEPH HENRY had published a detailed account of an electromagnetic telegraph in 1831, Morse did not know this and for several years believed that he had proposed the first one. By 1835 he had constructed his first operating telegraph. Two years later Leonard Gale, a teacher of science at the University of the City of New York where Morse taught art, introduced him to the work of Joseph Henry. Then Joseph Vail, a member of a wealthy family which owned an iron works in Morristown, New Jersey, offered to provide him with materials and labor to build his models. These men became his partners in business.

By 1838 Morse had developed the Morse code, and he asked Congress for an appropriation to build a telegraph line long enough to prove the practical use of his idea. Congress refused. For eight disappointing years Morse clung to his dream, and along with Vail, Gale, and Congressman F. O. J. Smith, a third partner, continued to promote his telegraph.

In 1843 he again asked Congress for money and for months and months waited for action to be taken. Finally on the night before Congress was to adjourn, Morse was granted $30,000 to construct a telegraph line from Baltimore to Washington. Jubilantly, Morse went to work, and on May 24, 1844, he tapped out his first message, "What Hath God Wrought!" D. H. J.

Mosaic virus see Virus

Moseley, Henry Gwyn-Jeffreys (1887-1915) Henry Moseley was an English physicist whose brilliant research in the field of X-RAY spectra of the elements was brought to an abrupt halt by his tragic death during World War I in the attack on Gallipoli.

Born at Weymouth, Dorset, Moseley was educated first at Eton and then at Trinity College, Oxford. Immediately following graduation, he accepted a post as lecturer in physics in Ernest Rutherford's laboratory at the University of Manchester, where he remained until wartime.

Henry Moseley's first research concerned RADIOACTIVITY. Then he began his spectacular research on the X-ray spectra of the ELEMENTS. He revealed the structure of the ELECTRON rings in almost all atoms so that the X-ray spectra of the elements could be arranged in a continuing series. Moseley's work made it possible to identify elements by continuously ordered numbers. His discovery was a vital contribution to the understanding of atomic structure. D. H. J.

Conversion Factors to Metric Measurement

Length

1 inch = 25.4 millimeters (mm) exactly
1 inch = 2.54 centimeters (cm) exactly
1 foot = 0.3048 meters (m) exactly
1 yard = 0.9144 meters (m) exactly
1 mile = 1.609344 kilometers (km) exactly

Area

1 square inch = 6.4516 square centimeters (cm^2) exactly
1 square foot = 0.092903 square meters (m^2)
1 square yard = 0.836127 square meters (m^2)
1 square acre = 0.404686 hectares (ha)
1 square mile = 2.58999 square kilometers (km^2)

Cubic Measure

1 cubic inch = 16.387064 cubic centimeters (cm^3) exactly
1 cubic foot = 0.0283168 cubic meters (m^3)
1 cubic yard = 0.764555 cubic meters (m^3)

US Liquid Measure

1 fluid ounce = 29.5735 milliliters (ml)
1 fluid ounce = 0.2957 deciliters (dl)
1 pint = 0.473176 liters (l)
1 gallon = 3.78541 liters (l)

US Dry Measure

1 pint = 0.550610 liters (l)
1 bushel = 35.2391 liters (l)

Weight

1 grain = 0.0647989 grams (g)
1 ounce = 28.3495 grams (g)
1 pound = 0.453592 kilograms (kg)
1 short ton = 0.907185 metric tons (t)
1 UK ton = 1.01605 metric tons (t)

Temperature

To convert Fahrenheit to Centigrade (Celsius) complete the following
equation. $(F° - 32) \times 5 \div 9 = C°$